BUILDING BETTER ESSAYS

Gina Baaklini Hogan
Citrus Community College

WADSWORTH
CENGAGE Learning

Australia • Brazil • Japan • Korea • Mexico • Singapore • Spain • United Kingdom • United States

WADSWORTH
CENGAGE Learning·

Building Better Essays
Gina Baaklini Hogan

Senior Publisher: Lyn Uhl

Director of Developmental
Studies: Annie Todd

Development Editor:
Marita Sermolins

Assistant Editor: Elizabeth Rice

Editorial Assistant:
Matthew Conte

Media Editor: Amy Gibbons

Marketing Coordinator:
Brittany Blais

Marketing Communications
Manager: Linda Yip

Art Director: Cate Barr

Print Buyer: Betsy Donaghey

Production Service: S4Carlisle
Publishing Services

Compositor: S4Carlisle
Publishing Services

For product information and
technology assistance, contact us at **Cengage Learning
Customer & Sales Support, 1-800-354-9706**

For permission to use material from this text or product,
submit all requests online at **cengage.com/permissions**
Further permissions questions can be emailed to
permissionrequest@cengage.com

Library of Congress Control Number: 2011944299

ISBN-13: 978-0-495-90517-2

ISBN-10: 0-495-90517-8

Wadsworth
20 Channel Center
Street Boston, MA
02210 USA

Cengage Learning is a leading provider of customized learning solutions with office locations around the globe, including Singapore, the United Kingdom, Australia, Mexico, Brazil, and Japan. Locate your local office at: **international
.cengage.com/region**

Cengage Learning products are represented in Canada by Nelson Education, Ltd.

For your course and learning solutions, visit
academic.cengage.com

Purchase any of our products at your local college store or at our preferred online store **www.ichapters.com**

Printed in the United States of America
1 2 3 4 5 6 7 15 14 13 12 11

Table of Contents

UNIT THREE: Building Loosely Structured Essays

Preface

BUILDING BLOCKS OF WRITING

Teaching writing in blocks as part of a building activity has provided my students with an easy to remember image that really helps them understand and apply good writing construction. This building process helps them see how each writing block sets the foundation for the next block; as a result, their confidence in writing grows the more they learn and write. In my classes, the first foundational block I teach is writing correct sentences; the second, writing effective paragraphs; and finally, writing effective essays. Just as real concrete foundations require specific raw materials (sand, water, cement, and gravel) that bind and mold together into a design, each writing building block (grammar, paragraphs, and essays) requires specific ingredients. For example, in grammar, to build a correct sentence you need nouns, verbs, prepositions, conjunctions, and other grammatical elements. When writing essays, the "ingredients" can include introduction paragraphs, thesis statements, supporting paragraphs, conclusion paragraphs, unity, and coherence.

As the third book of the *Building Better* series, *Building Better Essays* builds on students' knowledge of effective paragraph construction, covered in *Building Better Paragraphs*, to get them to the next step of putting paragraphs together successfully for coherent essays.

The *Building Better* series developed out of a need to help more students succeed in learning to write effectively. Teaching writing as a building activity where concepts build on each other has worked well in my developmental writing courses. This technique of "building writing" makes the writing process a manageable one because it allows students to practice each block separately, to see how it shapes subsequent blocks, and to increase their understanding and confidence along the way. In addition, this series also developed out of necessity—a need for cost-effective books that offer simple, accurate, student-friendly explanations. Many writing books present content in too complex a manner without enough opportunities for practice, or they present many topics that simply overwhelm the student. The *Building Better* series evolved with developmental students in mind; however, the textbooks are designed to be flexible enough that they can also be used as quick reference guides by all college students or writing instructors. Any student who needs help writing concise and clear essays can benefit from the pedagogy of *Building Better Essays*. Instructors looking for a rich focus on essay construction, easy-to-remember, simple explanations, and a variety of practice exercises will find it in *Building Better Essays*.

"This text is excellent compared to what I have used in the past. This book somehow is easy yet challenging. *Building Better Essays* only uses the necessities. Too many books have a lot of 'junk' in them. If I have students buy a text, I want to use the whole text and this is one where we could use the whole text."

—Marcia Cree, Long Beach City College

"*Building Better Essays* offers a simple and straightforward approach to the aspects of writing essays in various patterns. Each step and consideration in the writing process is explained and outlined in an effective way. Similar terms like "summary" and "paraphrase" are clearly distinguished and exercises are given that increase the students' understanding of the concepts being presented."

—Lynn Watson, Santa Rosa Junior College

HALLMARKS OF *BUILDING BETTER ESSAYS*

Tightly Structured and Loosely Structured Organization

Why organize patterns of essays into this unique categorization of tight and loose structure? Students struggle to figure out when and how to use patterns of writing. Yet, once Gina Hogan presented the patterns in her classes, she found that students who learn the tightly structured formats (like classification, cause or effect, and comparison or contrast) first gained great confidence and proficiency in the elements an essay should have. Then, when they transition to loosely structured essays (like narration, definition, and description), they retain their proficiency in keeping intact the basic structure of an essay (introduction paragraph with thesis statement, supporting paragraphs, and conclusion paragraph), yet they feel comfortable in adjusting the format and confident in their writing capabilities.

"I really like the idea that these non-specific patterns are distinguished from the specific patterns. Presenting the most difficult patterns (those that do not follow a prescribed or formal structure) as a unit is a plus. Too many texts present description and narration early; therefore, students do not acquire necessary, basic organizational skills."

—Kathleen Hoffman, Anoka Ramsey Community College-Cambridge Campus

Clarity and Consistency

Students who are being introduced to writing essays need a clear, consistent approach, so they can feel comfortable with a task they feel is insurmountable.

Developing writers are also usually developing readers, so all the concepts related to the writing process and writing patterns are carefully explained in an easy-to-remember manner.

> "*Building Better Essays* provides more thorough, yet more concisely worded, coverage of its topics and more effective models students can use to help improve their essay writing skills."
>
> —Jacob Agatucci, Cochise College

The chapters have a predictable flow that guides students through the writing process and, with each pattern, gently reminds students of what they have learned earlier as well as giving them new information to add to their writing skills arsenal. By providing students with the elements needed for an essay—introductory paragraph with thesis statement, supporting paragraphs with sufficient development, and concluding paragraph—for each pattern and by showing examples, students will feel supported to write their own essays. Realistic model essays demonstrate the kind of writing expected of students.

> "This text is very clearly worded and organized. The main split between the two major types of essays is innovative and creative, creating an unusual relationship among the subdivisions. Each chapter leads logically to the next and makes appropriate use of specific references to material in earlier chapters."
>
> —Patricia Gaston, West Virginia University–Parkersburg

> "I think one of the strongest components of *Building Better Essays* is the consistent organization. Students can follow every chapter and know the same format applies for each writing mode. They like that and really do learn especially after they have gotten used to the organization. I also appreciate the clear, but concise introduction paragraph in each chapter. Excellent discussion in a brief but clear manner."
>
> —Marcia Cree, Long Beach City College

Building Skills

Students participate in real, structured writing exercises throughout the chapters of *Building Better Essays*. The Building Skills exercises ask students to employ increased levels of effort and independence with varied opportunities to immediately practice newly learned skills, transitioning from identifying successful writing in practice sets to producing their own effective writing. Engaging, modern subjects in the Building Skills exercises serve to stimulate and encourage inventive writing from your students. Building Skills Together exercises promote collaborative work essential to writing and engagement among students.

> "I actually like all of the exercises—I usually ignore these parts of texts because they're boring. I like the use of YouTube and music . . . things the students are familiar with and interested in."
>
> —Jennifer Feller, Northern Virginia Community College

> "The editing task for the essays are excellent. Students absolutely need to be trained and need to practice this skill to be proficient. This book is the first where I have seen this particular task. All the topics for the essays are superb. This is the best part of the text. You choose very interesting topics and the essays really show a perfect example of the essay mode."
>
> —Marcia Cree, Long Beach City College

Memory Tips and Building Tips

Memory Tips present students with inventive, class-tested methods for remembering writing conventions and processes, many times with a unique mnemonic device. By highlighting important concepts, students can remember the writing steps and feel empowered when they set out to do the task on their own. Building Tips offer guidance to students by way of short, practical, and essential writing tips to apply to their writing.

> "The Memory Tips and Building Tips would be very helpful to my students in calling their attention to those items of content. It is especially helpful that they are not all the same or placed so as to become routine and lose effectiveness. Some are basic, but others require students to think and they re-emphasize the importance of materials and procedures just discussed."
>
> —James Sodon, St. Louis Community College-Florissant Valley

ADDITIONAL RESOURCES

Instructor's Resource Manual. By Gina Hogan of Citrus Community College. Streamline and maximize the effectiveness of your course preparation using such resources as complete answer keys to Building Skills and Building Skills Together exercises, as well as Teaching Tips designed to guide instructors through teaching each chapter.

Instructor Companion Site. The *Building Better* series Instructor Companion Website includes password-protected PowerPoint slides to accompany the text, additional quizzing, and a digital version of the Instructor's Resource Manual. Instructors can register for access to this resource at login.cengage.com.

Aplia for Basic Writing Levels 1 and 2. Founded in 2000 by economist and Stanford professor Paul Romer, Aplia is dedicated to improving learning by increasing student effort and engagement. Aplia is an online, auto-graded homework solution that keeps your students engaged and prepared for class, and has been used by more than 850,000 students at over 850 institutions. Aplia's online solutions provide developmental writing students with clear, succinct, and engaging writing instruction and practice to help them build the confidence they need to master basic writing and grammar skills. Aplia for Basic Writing: Level 1 (Sentence to Paragraph) and Aplia for Basic Writing: Level 2 (Paragraph to Essay) feature ongoing individualized practice, immediate feedback, and grades that can be automatically uploaded, so instructors can see where students are having difficulty (allowing for personalized assistance). Visit www.aplia.com/cengage for more details.

ACKNOWLEDGEMENTS

I am grateful to my parents, who instilled in me a strong love for learning and teaching. I deeply appreciate my husband and children for their enduring support and constant encouragement. I extend my ongoing gratitude to all college students, but especially developmental students, who allow me to be part of their academic journeys.

I am indebted more than I can say to Annie Todd at Cengage for her belief in the *Building Better* series and their author. I extend a huge thanks to Marita Sermolins, my development editor, for her expertise, dedication, and thoughtful supervision.

Much gratitude and appreciation is due the many colleagues around the country whose helpful feedback informed many parts of this book:

Jacob Agatucci, Cochise College

Matthew Allen, Wright College

Jackie Corbit, Cochise College

Marcia Cree, Long Beach City College

Lorraine Eadie, Berry College

Benjamin Eskew, Chaffey Community College

Jennifer Feller, Northern Virginia Community College-Woodbridge Campus

Patricia Gaston, West Virginia University-Parkersburg

Traci Gourdine, American River College

Kathleen Hoffman, Anoka Ramsey Community College-Cambridge Campus

Susan Hultgren, Cankdeska Cikana Community College

Maria Rankin-Brown, Pacific Union College

James Sodon, St. Louis Community College-Florissant Valley

Lynn Stewart, Cochise College

Lynn Watson, Santa Rosa Junior College

Ellen White-Khazrai, Paine College

Finally, my acknowledgement section is not complete without this: I dedicate this book to my wonderful family–Halim, Hiam, Bill, Remy, and Christopher. Your steadfast belief in me gives me wings to fly high!

UNIT ONE: Building the Foundation
The Writing Process

CONSIDER THESE SAMPLE college writing assignments.

Reflect on the recent class discussions about the readings on juvenile justice. Consider the issue of trying criminally violent juveniles or teenagers as adults. Discuss your viewpoint in a coherent essay of 500 words. Be sure to follow the MLA standards for manuscript format.

Reflect on the significance of the Industrial Revolution on our history. Write an essay comparing and contrasting the Industrial Revolution and the Second Industrial Revolution: The Technology Revolution.

Are you overwhelmed by the idea of assignments like these? You are certain to encounter assignments similar to these in your college courses, and this book will give you the simple building blocks you need to easily handle such college writing tasks. In college you are required to think and write about various concepts so you gain academic skills and understand the world around you. Essay writing is an expected college assignment, so the more you practice writing essays, the easier it gets.

WHY WRITE?

As a college student, you will be required to produce essays and research papers. These written assignments help you go on a journey of *discovery*—a discovery of yourself, your ideas and beliefs, and your world. Your writing shares your ideas with your audience who responds to you. That written communication gives you the power to entertain, inform, or even persuade others.

Your time spent learning how to write essays will also benefit you outside of college because it will help you learn to communicate effectively and clearly whether the circumstance is in school, on the job, or in your personal life. The ultimate goals of this book are:

- To help you explore your own thoughts and feelings about writing issues and concepts.
- To help you become an effective written communicator with the world around you.

THE WRITING PROCESS

Often, readers view only the completed product of a writer's work: the submitted paper. Readers rarely see what steps the writer has gone through to create a completed essay. In fact, a complete piece of writing does not happen all at once; instead, it goes through several steps, each designed to create a stronger, polished essay. These steps altogether make up the writing process, as shown in Figure 1.1.

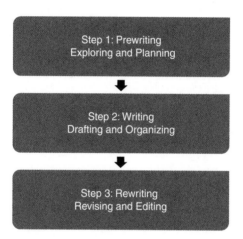

FIGURE 1.1. The Writing Process

Like any other process you use every day, such as washing the dishes, brushing your teeth, driving a car, or downloading music into your iPod, the writing process seems complicated and strange at first, but once you become familiar with the individual steps, you start doing them without thinking because they become second nature.

Most importantly, although writing generally goes through these three steps, it does not do so *chronologically*. Many times the writer may write a sentence only to change it by deleting or adding words; the writer may move a sentence to a better place in another part of the essay; or the writer may cross out whole paragraphs and start from scratch again. In other words, as a writer composes, often the three building steps of prewriting, writing, and rewriting are interconnected and overlap in that a step might happen by repeating another or while doing another. For this reason, the writing process is a **recursive** or repeating process, and it can stop, start, or go back and forth with any of the three steps. The thought of it as a series of steps makes it a manageable task. Figure 1.2 illustrates the recursive nature of the writing process where writers do not proceed in a straight line in their writing. Keep in mind, though, that writing does not have to be an overwhelming task.

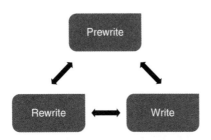

FIGURE 1.2. The Recursive Writing Process

Writing is a skill that improves with practice. Throughout the following chapters, you will become familiar with all the steps and requirements of effective writing. As you become more familiar with and master the different writing patterns, you will find yourself able to confidently evaluate and explain your thoughts about issues, ideas, and situations.

CHAPTER ONE: Prewriting and Planning Ideas

Generally, the writing process starts with a subject either generated by the writer or provided by the teacher and moves through the following steps: prewriting, writing, and rewriting.

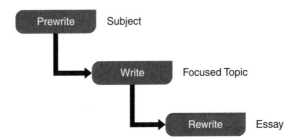

FIGURE 1.3. Writing Process Starts with a Subject

Many academic or professional writers admit that it is sometimes challenging to get started on writing. At times you may be asked to produce an essay about a subject of your interest. At other times, the **subject**—who or what the essay should be about—is assigned to you but may be intimidating, as you may not know much about it, it may be boring to you, or it may be something you may not have experienced.

The writing process is generally encouraged by a sense of urgency about the subject. The essay is something that has to be written not just to please the writing instructor or to get a good grade but because there is information or a point of view that you want to share with the reader. This urgency creates a relationship between you the writer and the readers or audience you are trying to reach and affect. Before you can reach your audience though, it is important to first understand your assignment's requirements and your purpose in sharing the information.

UNDERSTANDING YOUR ASSIGNMENT, PURPOSE, AND AUDIENCE

In college, the writing process often begins with an assignment about a specific subject. You may feel tempted to jump into writing, but it is better first to think about what your assignment, your purpose, and your audience are before you begin writing. In fact, these elements help inform your prewriting decisions about the subject.

Your **assignment** is the subject you are to write about and how you are required to do so. Many times, an assignment prompt given by your instructor will reveal exactly what you are to do. The first step in determining the assignment is to circle or reflect on key words or verbs, such as *illustrate, describe, narrate,* or *argue.* Then, once you have identified these words, make sure you understand what your instructor means by them. For example, suppose your instructor asks you to *illustrate* important political events during 1990. This could mean that you indicate and show the political events of that year and then explain their importance to politics and to the reader.

 **MEMORY TIP**

Consider the following common verbs used in essay prompts and what they require of the writer.

ANALYZE To separate something into parts and discuss, examine, or interpret each part.

CLASSIFY To put something into a category with things of a similar type.

COMPARE To examine two or more things and to show their similarities.

CONTRAST To examine two or more things and show their differences.

CRITICIZE To analyze and make reasoned judgments about something.

DEFINE To give the meaning of a term or concept.

DESCRIBE To give the physical or nonphysical qualities or characteristics of something.

EVALUATE To give a reasoned opinion about something, usually in terms of the quality of a particular work, idea, or person.

ILLUSTRATE To give examples or to describe something.

INTERPRET To comment upon something or explain its meaning.

PERSUADE To urge or influence the audience to embrace your point of view.

PROVE To argue a position by supporting your claims with factual evidence.

Beyond understanding what is being asked of you, ask yourself these questions to focus on what the specific requirements are for your assignment:

- What subject does the assignment focus on?
- Is there a word limit, a sentence limit, or a page limit?
- When is the assignment due?
- Are you expected to work on it only at home, only in class, or both?
- Are you expected to write it on your own or with others?
- Are you allowed to revise your work?

Once you have determined the requirements for your assignment, consider the **purpose**, or why you are writing this essay, aside from the fact that it has been assigned. Your purpose is what you hope to share or to accomplish in writing this essay. It may be that you want to inform, entertain, or persuade the reader. Whatever purpose you decide to adopt will determine the ideas you explore that give direction to your subject. Identifying and understanding your purpose as early as possible in the writing process saves you countless hours of rework later in the drafting cycle. Consider the following questions to determine your purpose:

- Should you **inform** the reader by presenting information or your feelings about the subject?
- Should you **entertain** the reader by providing humorous anecdotes, short stories, or real events about the subject?
- Should you **persuade** the reader by presenting strong evaluations or opinions about the subject?

BUILDING SKILLS 1-1: Determining Main Purpose

For each topic, determine a purpose and explain your reason for it. Your purpose may be to inform, entertain, or persuade your audience.

1. **Topic:** Identity theft
   Purpose: _____

2. **Topic:** Approving the smoking ban on college campuses
   Purpose: _____

3. **Topic:** A person's sense of pride
   Purpose: _____

4. **Topic:** The disadvantages of student loans
   Purpose: _____

5. **Topic:** The dark side of fame
   Purpose: _____

You also need to consider who will be reading your essay—your **audience**. Knowing your intended audience helps you decide on the extent of your explanation, your writing style, and word choice. For example, when you describe a party to your coworker or friends, the details you present and how you say them will be different with each audience. You may tell your friends more specific details than you tell your coworker. Moreover, you may use slang with your friends but formal language with your coworker. In any case, you meet the needs of the audience by changing your language and presentation. To identify your audience for a topic, develop an **audience profile** by asking the following questions:

- Who will read my essay? Is it just my teacher or other students in my class? How much knowledge might my teacher, classmates, or others have about my topic?
- If not my teacher or classmates, who else might be interested in my topic? What knowledge about my topic would my audience already have?
- What demographics describe my audience: age, gender, religious beliefs, income status, social status, or educational background?
- Will my readers expect formal or informal language?
- Are the readers supportive or unsympathetic to the topic?

BUILDING SKILLS 1-2: Determining Audience

Identify an audience who would be interested in reading about the following topics and explain why that audience would be interested.

1. **Topic:** Movie review
   Audience: _____

2. **Topic:** Essay exam in a literature class
   Audience: _____

3. **Topic:** College campus highlights
   Audience: _____

4. **Topic:** Crimes in your neighborhood
   Audience: _____

5. **Topic:** Art club fundraiser invitation
   Audience: _____

FOCUSING ON POINT OF VIEW

Once you determine the assignment's subject and requirements, your purpose for writing, and your intended readers, consider the perspective or point of view from which you should write the essay. Specifically, what pronoun or person you should use throughout the essay to inform, entertain, or persuade the audience.

 BUILDING TIP

You can write using any of the following points of view:

- **First-person** point of view uses the pronouns *I* or *we*.
- **Second-person** point of view uses the pronouns *you* or *your.*
- **Third-person** point of view uses the pronouns *she, he, it, they, him, her* or *names of people.*

Because point of view shows the writer's relationship to the subject or from whose perspective the subject is being explained or described, it should stay consistent throughout the essay.

If you are sharing a personal story, use the **first-person** point of view of *I* or *we* because it is a personal story that you are sharing.

> I could tell something bad would happen that day because of what I had seen and heard. I was not surprised when I heard the townspeople talk about the washed-up sailor.

If you are writing instructions or how-to essays, use the **second-person** point of view or *you* and *your.*

> To make French fries, first you must wash the potato head. Then, you must peel the skin off each potato head, making sure you cut out any bad spots without trimming too much. Next, you slice the potatoes lengthwise. After this, you fry them in hot oil for one minute.

 MEMORY TIP

The second-person point of view is most appropriate for how-to essays, but is not appropriate for formal or academic essays simply because it is very difficult to write from this point of view without confusing readers, who might think the author is addressing them. It is best to avoid using *you* language in your essays unless it is required by your instructor.

If you are explaining something from a detached position, use the **third-person** point of view or refer to your subjects by name or by pronouns such as *it, he, she, they, him, her,* and/or *them.* Most college essays require the use of the detached third-person perspective.

Romeo, one of Shakespeare's most memorable characters, attends a ball at the Capulet house where he meets and falls in love with Juliet. After the ball, in what is now called the "balcony scene," he sneaks into the Capulet courtyard and overhears Juliet on her balcony vowing her love to him in spite of her family's hatred of the Montagues. He makes himself known to her, and they agree to be married. With the help of Father Lawrence, who hopes to reconcile the two families through their children's union, they are secretly married the next day.

WHAT IS PREWRITING?

Determining your assignment, purpose, audience, and point of view can help to inform your decisions about the subject of your essay. Those decisions guide your process of exploring and generating the ideas you need to inform, persuade, or entertain the reader. This process of exploring and generating is the prewriting step in the writing process.

When you **prewrite**, you brainstorm or consider your knowledge of the subject to help produce ideas about it. Generally, this step occurs before you start writing so that you stimulate your thinking about the subject; however, you may use it anytime during your writing to consider or reconsider ideas. Really, you think about writing *before* and *while* actually doing it.

In addition, prewriting helps you develop more interest about your subject. The more interested you are in your subject, the more invested and engaged you are in sharing your information and writing your essay. The prewriting step helps you to:

- explore your knowledge
- generate ideas about a subject
- narrow the subject to a specific topic
- plan the organizing pattern

> ### ✂ BUILDING TIP
> If you are assigned a subject, it is helpful to put the subject at the top of the blank page before you begin prewriting. This helps you to focus on the subject and inspire a rush of ideas.

EXPLORING AND GENERATING IDEAS

The exploring and generating of ideas occurs before you start and sometimes while you are writing, and it helps you discover what you may or may not know about the subject. It inspires you to consider your thoughts and feelings about the subject, which in turn helps you to shape ideas you need for writing. Any of these methods can help you to explore and generate ideas:

- free writing
- questioning or "big six" questions
- visual mapping
- reading/journaling/discussing

Use any of these techniques to investigate ideas at any time during your writing. You may use more than one technique to prewrite, or you may use some to build on others. You may begin with free writing and then take those generated ideas and map them visually in an outline form or use them for journaling. In other words, the prewriting techniques are recursive in that one can build upon another; therefore, you may use any or all of the prewriting techniques for producing and developing ideas about a subject.

✖ BUILDING TIP

Since all prewriting techniques are about exploring ideas or digging into what you may know about a subject, do not concern yourself with proper grammar or spelling as you prewrite. Your prewritten ideas need to be clear to *only* you, the potential writer, so be comfortable in expressing your prewriting ideas.

Free Writing

As its name implies, with **free writing**, you write *freely* and continuously for a specific amount of time, usually five to fifteen minutes, without concern for grammar errors, spelling, or punctuation. You are recording your thoughts as they occur to you, regardless of form or logic. As you free write, you may draw pictures and symbols, use numbers, or use words from another language. You might prefer typing or free typing rather than writing ideas. Whether you free write or free type, the goal is to write (or type) without stopping until your time is up or until you run out of ideas. In other words, babble on paper until you cannot do so any more. Free writing resembles a warm-up you might do before exercising. It gets you started on writing by helping you collect initial thoughts and ideas.

There are two types of free writing:

- **Unfocused free writing:** This is writing or typing freely about anything that comes to your mind. No specific subject or topic is assigned for an unfocused free write. There is no correct way to do this, so try a variation of these steps:
  - Begin with a blank computer screen and a watch (or the clock on the computer). You might use a pen and paper instead—remember that free writing involves generating words, not correcting them or getting just the right word.
  - Set a time for yourself. Try one, five, or ten minutes.
  - Begin to type or write about anything that comes into your head. Do not stop until the time is up.
  - Then review what you have written. Are there words you like? Ideas that might work?

Consider this example of an unfocused free write.

My mom worries me cause I don't know what she wants from me she yells at me all the time and is never happy around me. Why am I writing about this? the teacher wants me to write about anything but I'm hungry cause the sandwich I had for lunch did not fill me up. Mybe after class I'll go to Jack's Pizza Place and have me a large pizza hold the anciovies please! Those anchioves are slimy! Wow my fingers are getting greasy just thinking about the stringy oily cheese on the pizza. Or maybe I should just go home and have mom's cooking I think she making a special dinner tonite for my brothers birthday. Oh no I need to get my bro a gift! How could I have forgot? Me and my brother are cool we undersand each other. Hey mabe I'll get him those running shoes he liked at the mall. He deserves them he works so hard and he helps me when I get into fights with mom. Yeah I think I'll go by the mall first then home to mom and bro. I hope mom makes her famous lasagna I do like her cooking even if we don't agree all the time on everything. Her food is the best and there's none like it. Yeah my mom is cool I guess. Maybe Ill buy my mom something at the mall too. . .

This student's unfocused free writing exposes several ideas going through that person's mind. For example, he could write about:

- Jack's Pizza Place
- his relationship with his mom
- his relationship with his brother
- his family's connection over mom's food

- **Focused free writing.** This is writing freely about a specific subject or topic. Focused free writing works best when your instructor indicates a specific topic, although sometimes you may use a topic you are especially interested in writing about. Try following these steps:
  - Put a topic of your choice, or the topic of your assignment, at the top of a blank screen or page.
  - Set a time limit and begin typing or writing. Write down things that seem to be related to the topic. Do not worry about order of ideas or grammatical correctness.
  - When the time is up, look over what you have written. Pull out ideas and phrases you want to use later.
  - Practice putting your free writing into outline form. If you were to use the writing to begin a paper, which points would you make first? Second?

Consider this example of focused free writing with *books* as its subject.

Books

People sometimes keep all the books they have ever read. They put them on tables, on their nitestands, on their shelves, or on the floor. They may never be read again, but they sit there, take up space, fall apart, or become a fire hazard. ebooks, or electronic books that are downloaded into electronic devices, I think are the way to go for lovers of books like me.

With all this internet stuff, people can buy, store, and read books electronically using the Kindle or Nook. These devices can be taken anywhere and allow access to an entire library of books with the touch of a button! I can download classics like *Pride and Prejudice* or the first chapter of any book for free! If the user likes the first chapter and wants to buy the book, he can do so with one click and the entire book will be downloaded within sixty seconds and saved for a long time.

Ebooks and edevices like my Kindle (or Nook) have changed the way people read and the way people deal with books. (my sister as an example of sister) People spend more time in front of screens and less time in front of printed books; therefore, ebooks are good for the environment. They save trees! Also, ebooks are ageless and do not burn or fall apart.

This student's focused free write about books exposes the importance of e-books.

BUILDING SKILLS 1-3: Focused Free writing

Do focused free write (or free type) sessions on two of the phrases below. For each phrase you choose, spend ten minutes free writing. Remember to write or type nonstop for the whole ten minutes.

- The three best products ever invented
- A movie or book that changed the way you look at life
- The messages in hip-hop (or any other genre) music

Based on your free writing, what would you focus an essay on if you were assigned to write about one of these topics?

Questioning ("Big Six" Questions)

People learn and process information in many different ways. Some learn best by seeing, others by hearing, and still others by doing. Some prefer a defined structure, whereas others think best when there are no constraints. For those who like structure, the **"big six" questions** offer an easy framework for generating ideas.

Sometimes when you ask specific questions, the answers you get may trigger your mind into thinking about the subject or into thinking about it in a different way than you would have otherwise. The "big six" questions, sometimes also called reporter's questions, are used by journalists to find out more about an event or incident before they report on it. These six questions can also help you investigate your interest in a specific subject. The questions are:

- Who?
- What?
- Where?
- When?
- How?
- Why?

Consider this student's example about sports as the subject:

> Sports
> Who: MVP player Kobe Bryant and Shaquille O'Neal
> What: their feud and their split
> Where: NBA's Lakers Team—on and off the court
> When: 1996 to 2004
> How: offensive verbal remarks and snubs
> Why: personal differences and arguments over roles on team

After answering the six questions, this student felt most comfortable with the answer to the *Who* and *Why* questions, so she picked as her focused essay topic Kobe Bryant and his feud with O'Neal. In other words, a combination of two of the "big six" answers allowed her to produce her focused topic.

BUILDING SKILLS 1-4: "Big Six" Questions

Use the "big six" questions (*who, what, where, when, how,* and *why*) to explore the following subjects. For each of the subjects, answer all six questions; then, identify the answer that you are most comfortable with to use as the basis for an essay.

- Music
- Vacation
- Money
- College

Visual Mapping: Lists, Outlines, and Cluster Maps

For many, a visual representation of ideas or a graphic organizer works better. You can "see" ideas develop creatively and graphically instead of writing long sentences. For this, you can use lists, outlines, or cluster maps.

Lists make it easy to see individual ideas as they emerge one at a time. This method works well for writers who like to organize thoughts or ideas linearly in lists. Suppose you are listing ideas about the subject of good college study habits:

> Good college study habits
> – manage time well
> – take good notes
> – organize papers and books
> – keep a good attendance record

Which one of the listed items interests you most as a writer if this were your prewriting list? Isolate that one item that interests you the most and use it as a basis for developing an essay.

BUILDING SKILLS 1-5: Using Lists

For each subject, list ideas you relate to the subject. Then, for each subject, isolate one idea to use for writing an essay.

- Gossip   - Apologies   - Greed

Outlines are extended lists of ideas that make it easier to see the flow of thoughts. They can be **informal**, with creative ways of representing ideas, or **formal**, with complete sentences and Roman numerals.

👆 MEMORY TIP

- **Informal outlines** are also called **topic outlines** because they show ideas developed in a few words.
- **Formal outlines** are also called **sentence outlines** because they show ideas developed in complete sentences.

Informal outlines are useful in seeing brief, general structures of the thesis statement and topic sentences and supporting ideas whereas formal outlines offer specific and expanded structures of support for the thesis statement and topic sentences. Sometimes formal outlines may be useful later in the writing process, after you have written a rough draft, because they can help you see how the specific parts of your essay work together or bring order to your thoughts. The guidelines for constructing an outline are as follows:

1. Put the focused topic or thesis statement at the top of the page.
2. Number the main ideas with roman numerals (I, II, III, IV. . .), indent, and number the second-level ideas with capitalized letters followed by numbers and so on.

Informal (Topic) Outline	Formal (Sentence) Outline

Thesis statement: Construction on college campus affects parking.
I. Earlier times for students
  - Arrive hours before class
  - Long walk to class
II. More competition for parking spots
  - Violent fights
  - Car accidents
III. Students park in neighborhood streets
  - Block residents
  - Illegal parking
	Thesis statement: The construction of the new college campus softball field has eliminated a parking structure for 150 cars, which has resulted in several dire problems.
	I. Students have to get to campus earlier to find parking spots.
	  A. Students sometimes have to get to campus two to three hours before classes start.
	    1. Students have to walk long distances from where they parked to get to class.
	    2. They are late to class.
	II. There is more competition for fewer parking spots.
	  A. There are only two parking structures available now.
	    1. Tensions rise as more students are vying for fewer parking spots.
	    2. There have been four violent attacks and three car accidents in the last semester.
	III. Students park in neighborhood streets.
	  A. Residents are angry.
	    1. The streets are crowded with cars that block driveway access.
	    2. Some cars are parked illegally resulting in the city issuing many illegal parking tickets.
	Conclusion: The parking problems caused by the construction of the softball field require that college administrators address them if they do not want to lose students to neighboring colleges.

BUILDING SKILLS 1-6: Completing Outlines

Fill in the missing parts of the following essay outlines. Some parts are provided for you, but depending on your individual experiences and views, your answers will vary.

1. Informal Outline
   Thesis statement: There are several alternatives to fast food when it comes to feeding a family.
   I. _____
   II. _____
   III. _____

2. Formal Outline
   Thesis statement: There are several negative effects of credit cards.
   I. One negative effect is one has more money to spend.
      A. _____
         1. _____
         2. _____
      B. _____
         1. _____
         2. _____
   II. A second negative effect is one has more opportunity to go into debt.
      A. _____
         1. _____
         2. _____
      B. _____
         1. _____
         2. _____
   III. The worst effective is the potential for identity theft.
      A. _____
         1. _____
         2. _____
      B. _____
         1. _____
         2. _____

Clusters or **maps** are visual shapes like circles and lines that show how ideas are related. With both clustering and mapping, place the major idea in the middle of the page with a circle around it, "bubble" in related ideas around the main one, and connect them to the main idea. Figure 1.4 shows an example of a cluster.

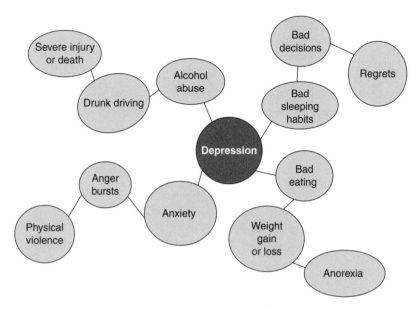

FIGURE 1.4. Cluster Example about Depression

You can keep branching or bubbling out from the ideas you have until you feel that you have fully explored your subject. Then, you can choose the bubbles that you are most comfortable with to elaborate on in an essay.

BUILDING SKILLS 1-7: Using Clusters

For each subject, prewrite related ideas by clustering. Then, isolate a few ideas for each subject to use for writing an essay.

- YouTube
- Smoking
- Challenges

BUILDING SKILLS 1-8: Listing, Outlining, and Clustering

In a group or with a classmate, prewrite on one of the subjects listed here by using the following techniques sequentially: listing first, clustering second, and outlining third.

- Web sites
- Dating
- Grades
- Loyalty

Reading, Journaling, and Discussing

Sometimes, especially in advanced composition classes, a good way to start the writing process is to **read** a newspaper or magazine article, a short story, or an article on the Internet. As you read, take notes on the main ideas or unusual words or expressions and mark the reading with comments as they occur to you. These notes and comments will be the beginnings of your ideas about what subject you should write about.

In some instances, **journaling** or keeping a journal is a good way to get ideas. Keeping a journal allows you to record thoughts, opinions, or impressions on paper and offers you a chance to practice writing without worrying about rules or the audience. It is good to commit to writing in your journal every day for a few minutes to jot down personal ideas; things you have learned in class or at work; controversial issues in your city, state, or country; or interesting facts from newspapers or television shows. Really, you can write about any subject that appeals to you. It is a good way to reflect and grow as a thinker and ultimately as a writer. In some classes, you may be asked to keep formal journals in which you summarize and respond to a text you have read. These classes require your active involvement with the reading and rely on sharing experiences and feedback with your classmates or in your writing.

For some journaling assignments, you may be required to write summaries about what you read. A **summary** is a brief description of the main events in the story. It needs to include only the chronological highlights (the beginning, middle, and end) of what happened. A summary doesn't express your opinion as a writer, but instead retells the key events in your own words.

Discussing is the act of talking over your ideas with friends, relatives, classmates, or teachers. Sometimes someone else will have a different way of looking at things that will help you develop more ideas. Be sure to record notes from the discussion so that you can use them later for your writing. *Note:* In literature courses or advanced English courses, you may be asked to do all three—reading, journaling, and discussing—before you are assigned a subject to write about. These classes rely on your engaging with a reading and sharing your experiences and feedback.

BUILDING SKILLS 1-9: Reading, Journaling, and Discussing

Read any essay, article, or short story and follow these directions.

1. As you read it, underline unusual words and make comments in the margins.

2. Write a journal responding (negatively or positively) to the reading.

3. Share your journal entry with classmates during an in-class discussion.

❚ BUILDING SKILLS TOGETHER 1-1: Using All the Prewriting Techniques

As a group, choose one of the subjects listed below. Then, explore it on separate paper by following the listed sequence of prewriting techniques.

Subjects:

- Drug use
- Gang membership
- Extreme sports
- Traditions

Subject Chosen: _____

Prewriting Techniques:

- Free write
- "Big six" questions
- Listing or clustering
- Informal or formal outline
- Reading and journaling (Find an article on the Internet or through your college' library related to your chosen subject.)

NARROWING THE SUBJECT AND PLANNING THE IDEAS

Prewriting helps you explore and generate ideas about the subject, so you can discover what you would like to build on in your writing. You use your prewriting ideas to **narrow** or **focus** the subject, so you can develop one main specific idea or **focused topic** in your essays.

Narrowing the subject is like taking a picture with a camera. The subject is the wide-angle lens, and the individual element you have chosen to zoom in on is your topic. Suppose you are taking a picture of a garden; then, your wide-angle shot or subject is the garden, but the narrow-angle shot or topic is the red rose in the center of the garden.

To narrow a subject, first look at the sentences or words in your prewriting and circle or isolate the ones you like, or that you think might work. The next step is to group similar ideas or words together to see what fits with what and where. Then, look at the connected ideas and see what seems to be the one focus that emerges. You may not use every idea from your prewriting, or you may find that

> ### 👆 MEMORY TIP
>
> Different teachers may call an essay's specific idea by different terms.
> They may refer to it in any of the following ways:
>
> - writer's opinion
> - main idea
> - key focus
> - argument
> - focused idea
> - narrowed topic
> - main lesson
>
> - main point
> - main impression
> - dominant idea
> - dominant impression
> - central idea
> - controlling idea
>
> This book uses the term **focused topic** to define an essay's specific focus.

you do not have enough ideas. In any case, just by looking at your prewriting and making associations between ideas, you will have a better sense of what your focus could be and how the other ideas could work as support for it. If you find that you need more ideas, do more prewriting using the same technique as the one you used before, or using one of the other prewriting techniques. Consider the example in Figure 1.5.

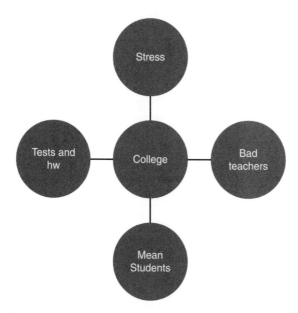

FIGURE 1.5. Narrowing the Subject of *College*

The subject or general wide-angle shot is college, and the individual ideas about college or specific close-up shots may include *stress, mean students, bad teachers,* and *tests and homework.* Now, select one of those ideas. The bubble you choose to focus on from the cluster is the topic you will write about in relation to the subject.

Suppose you isolated *bad teachers* as a topic. Now, to support and develop the topic of bad college teachers, you can use some of the other ideas in the cluster such as *many tests and homework assignments, inattention to mean students,* and *stressful classroom environment.* Reflect on what the detail ideas (tests and homework, mean students, and stressful environment) may tell you about bad teachers to narrow the topic further, so you can express a specific opinion about it. From your reflection on the ideas you isolated, you may produce the following **focused topic**: *several factors make for bad college teachers.* You could create a new cluster for stress to develop more ideas on the topic of bad college teachers, as in Figure 1.6.

Suppose you liked and isolated mean students as your focus or topic; now you can write an essay on that and use new ideas for details, or perhaps use some of the other ideas in the cluster, such as cheating on tests and homework, as details for the **focused topic** of *what mean students do in college classes,* as shown in Figure 1.7.

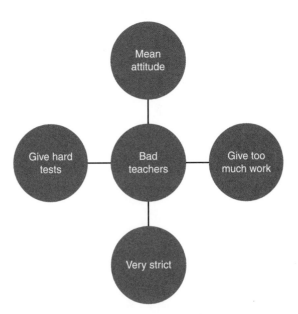

FIGURE 1.6. Narrowing the Subject of *Bad Teachers*

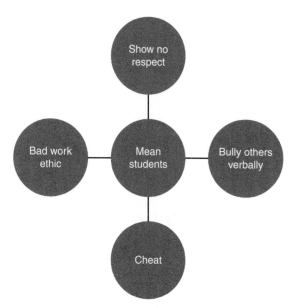

FIGURE 1.7.   Narrowing the Subject of *What Mean Students Do in College Classes*

BUILDING SKILLS 1-10: Narrowing a Subject into a Focused Topic

Refer back to Building Skills Together 1-1. Review your prewriting answers for the topic you have chosen to explore. Then, write a sentence that reflects a clear focus about your topic.

_____

_____

_____

_____

♦ BUILDING SKILLS TOGETHER 1-2: Prewriting Techniques

In a small group, work through the following prompts:

1. Use any or all prewriting techniques—free writing, "big six" questions, listing, or clustering—to prewrite on the following subject: *Social networking sites* like Facebook and Twitter.

2. Next, choose one person to write down ideas, with each group member contributing at least one idea.

3. Then, discuss your prewrite about the topic and identify interesting connections among the ideas that have been written down.

4. From these ideas, narrow the subject to one clear focus. Write a few possible focused sentences about the subject; then, choose the one all group members agree on.

5. Share your prewriting and focused topic with the class.

CHAPTER TWO: Writing Essays

In Chapter One, you learned about the prewriting step in the writing process. In this chapter, you will learn about the second step in the writing process where you actually compose a draft of an essay using the topic and ideas you generated from your prewriting. Writing the essay helps you bring together and organize ideas into a clear structure that flows logically and makes sense.

Many writers go through multiple drafts for their essays, and the first attempt at drafting is called a **rough draft** because it tends to be a basic, unrefined, and unpolished version. It allows you to produce an initial structured format of your ideas to see if they support your topic or if you need more development. It includes unclear sentences, awkward phrases, misspelled words, and extraneous ideas; however, it is something you can build on and improve.

DRAFTING AN ESSAY

An **essay** is a collection of paragraphs, typically between four and six paragraphs, but can vary in length depending on the assignment. The number of paragraphs is not as important as how these paragraphs function together to show the writer's opinion. In other words, the content conveyed in those paragraphs is most essential. Both paragraphs and essays are structured around three main parts. As you move from paragraph to essay, the name of each part changes.

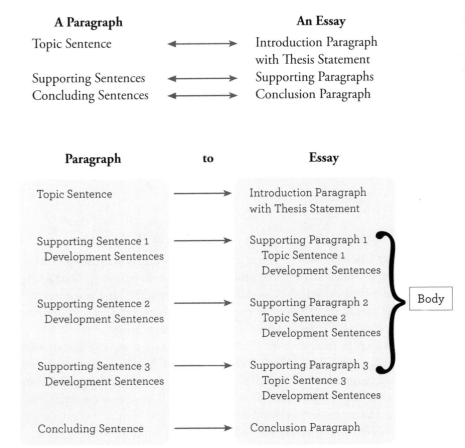

A Paragraph		**An Essay**
Topic Sentence	⟷	Introduction Paragraph with Thesis Statement
Supporting Sentences	⟷	Supporting Paragraphs
Concluding Sentences	⟷	Conclusion Paragraph

Thus, the strong parallel between the organization of a paragraph and an essay leads to the consideration that the paragraph shares similar structural elements with the essay. See pages 28–29 for a side-by-side comparison of a paragraph and essay on the same topic.

An essay includes an introduction, body, and conclusion. There is no perfect length for an essay as it depends on the assignment and your purpose in writing, but essays are generally composed of multiple paragraphs. Some college courses require a five-paragraph essay. The important thing to remember is that regardless of length, all essays include an introduction paragraph, body paragraphs, and a conclusion paragraph.

My People's Influence

Paragraph

There are several people who have influenced me as I pursued my educational goals. The first person is my older sister, Char. She is always willing to help me when I need it: in fact, I always have her reread the papers that I have to write. She always gives good advice that makes my papers more interesting. She used to be upset with me for my grammatical errors, but now she is amazed that I write so well. Another person who has influenced me has been my high school sports coach, Miguel. He always asks me how I'm doing in my schoolwork, and if I tell him that I'm getting a C in one of my classes, he asks me how I'm going to bring that grade up. Since he has been my coach, he has ways of making me try harder in my studies. If I need any help with anything, even outside of school, he is there to help me out. I know that he will do his best to help me when I need any help. The most influential person who has helped me in accomplishing my educational goals is my girlfriend, Laura. She has pushed me the most in my studies. She picks me up when I'm down on myself and when I stress out. She will tell me if my writing sounds catchy or not, so I can make corrections as needed. She's there to keep me in check. In addition, she is always there to give me a big hug and words

Supporting sentence 1 with a transition

Supporting sentence 2 with a transition

Supporting sentence 3 with a transition

Essay

Many people do not understand how difficult pursuing an education can be, and many families take no pride in their loved ones' education. On the other hand, some regard education as a high accomplishment and take great interest in their loved ones' education. I am lucky in having my family's and friends' great support, and, along the way, several people have become great influences on the pursuit of my education.

The first person to influence me is my older sister, Char. She is a graduate of Cal Poly, Pomona, with dual degrees in Business and Agriculture. Despite her dyslexia, she was able to accomplish a lot in her life, and she is my inspiration. She is always willing to help me when I need it: in fact, I always have her reread my papers that I have to write. She always gives me good advice that makes my papers more interesting. She used to get on me for my grammatical errors a lot, but since I've taken English classes in college, she is amazed at how well I write now.

Another person who has influenced me has been my high school sports coach, Miguel. He always asks me how I'm doing in my schoolwork, and if I tell him that I'm getting a "C" in one of my classes, he asks me how I'm going to bring that grade up.

Thesis statement

Topic sentence of supporting paragraph 1

Topic sentence of supporting paragraph 2

My People's Influence (continued)

Concluding sentence

of encouragement. My sister, coach, and my girl-friend are the people who have influenced me in the pursuit of my educational goals.

He is my mentor, and to him education is the key to a better life and a wise mind. Since he's been my coach, he has ways of making me try harder in my studies. If I need any help with anything, even outside of school, he is there to help me out. He always reminds me of the promise I made to him about finishing my bachelor's degree.

Topic sentence of supporting paragraph 3

The most influential person who has helped me in accomplishing my educational goals is my girlfriend, Laura. She's had a hard life as an orphan, but through it all her focus never wavered, and she accomplished her goal. She just finished her degree in nursing after years of working two jobs to pay her tuition. She understands how hard it can be sometimes, but she has pushed me the most in my studies. She picks me up when I'm down on myself and when I stress out. She will help me study for tests or tell me if my writing sounds catchy or not, so I can make corrections as needed. She's there to keep me in check. In addition, she is always there to give me a big hug and words of encouragement.

Restatement of thesis

I am fortunate to have my sister, coach, and girl-friend as the people who have influenced me in the pursuit of my educational goals. They have made it easier for me to achieve academically. In the words of George Eliot, "What do we live for, if it is not to make life less difficult to each other?"

Final observation

Introduction Paragraph

The **introduction** is the first paragraph in the essay, and its purpose is to introduce the reader to what the essay is about specifically. The length of the introduction can vary, depending on your topic and purpose, but it accomplishes several things:

- Attracts or **"hooks"** the reader's attention
- Provides **specific remarks** about the subject
- States the **thesis statement** and *may* state the **forecasting statement**

An introduction moves the reader from general to specific ideas. It may begin with a sentence or sentences that introduce the discussion and "hook" the reader's attention, but by the end of the introductory paragraph, the reader should understand the essay's main focus. Generally, most introductions may follow this general diagram:

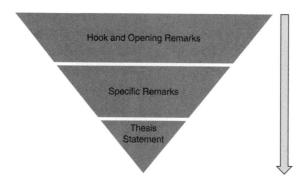

The Hook

The **hook** is a sentence or sentences at the beginning of the introductory paragraph that start the discussion and attract readers' attention, so they keep reading. There are a number of ways to write the hook to get readers' attention:

1. **General scenario or historical background information.** You can offer a short story, anecdote, or several common-knowledge factual sentences about your topic in the first sentences before your thesis statement.

> We have an Oscars ceremony once a year to tell rich people how great they are for standing in front of a camera for millions of dollars a week playing roles of brave firemen or conscionable doctors. For entertaining the masses they get paid exorbitant amounts of money and are given great recognition, while those who truly risk their lives every day to keep others safe are not given a second glance. We should give awards to those who are real heroes every day, who risk their lives for others.

2. **Definition.** You can start with a definition of a word that relates to your discussion. Consider the following opening sentences taken from a longer introductory paragraph.

> Actors are not true heroes. Heroes are real people who save lives regardless of the danger to their own safety.

3. **Quotation.** Somewhere in the introductory sentences, you can use a quote from someone famous, from an old saying, or from a slogan, song, or movie.

> According to William Shakespeare, "All the world's a stage, and all the men and women merely players; they have their exits and their entrances; and one man in his time plays many parts," so why not recognize these players on stage who entertain us with their heroic acting? After all, they may make their exits all too soon.

4. **Shocking statement or question.** In your first sentence, use a shocking statement or ask a question to grab the readers' attention.

> Shocking statement: My favorite movie hero has died from a drug overdose. He left me wondering what I ever saw in him that was heroic. A hero is someone who makes a difference and lives the values he espouses.
>
> Question: Should famous actors be recognized as heroes? Just because they are talented at impersonating characters may not mean they are of good character themselves. A hero is...

After the hook sentences are presented, you may offer a few common informational remarks about the specific topic of your essay and move the reader toward your main focus: the thesis statement.

Thesis Statement

The foundation of an effective essay is a strong thesis statement. The introduction includes a thesis statement, which indicates the essay's topic and the writer's specific opinion about the topic. The thesis statement is a statement of opinion and not a statement of fact. A **fact** is something that can be verified or proven.

Sixty-three percent of college students work while attending college.

Can you confirm that number from a survey in a book? Yes. Then this is a fact; it cannot be a topic sentence because you cannot explain a fact. An **opinion** requires that its writer show you why he or she feels, believes, or thinks that way because it is not based on fact, and it is not verifiable. Each one of us has his or her way of looking at things.

Maggie is the most beautiful girl in the world.

Does everyone in the world agree to this? No. The writer may have this feeling, but someone else might think Maggie is the ugliest girl in the world. Since someone can disagree with this feeling, this is an opinion. Now, the writer has to share with others why Maggie is the most beautiful girl, and they may agree or disagree.

⚒ BUILDING TIP

The thesis statement offers an **opinion** or a narrowed focus about the topic. This narrowed focus is also called the **focused topic** of the essay. The focused topic is what the writer will explain or show in the essay.

You may place your thesis statement anywhere in the beginning or middle of the introduction, although generally it is placed at the end of the introduction, after you have hooked the reader and given some specific remarks about your topic. Wherever you place your thesis statement, it always tells readers what to expect in your essay. In one sentence, a thesis statement should:

- State your opinion or **focused topic** about the subject.
- Indicate what **writing pattern** is used for organizing supporting details.

> ### 👆 MEMORY TIP
>
> Different teachers may call an essay's thesis statement by different terms. They may refer to it in any of the following ways:
>
> | | |
> |---|---|
> | ■ writer's opinion | ■ narrowed topic |
> | ■ main point | ■ main lesson |
> | ■ main idea | ■ main impression |
> | ■ key focus | ■ dominant idea or impression |
> | ■ argument | ■ central idea |
> | ■ focused idea | ■ controlling idea |
>
> This book uses the term **focused topic** to define an essay's specific focus.

To write an effective thesis statement, consider your purpose for the topic because that helps you determine how best to explain it to your readers. Ask yourself:

■ What feelings or thoughts do I have about the topic?
■ What kinds of thoughts about this topic do I want to share with my audience?
■ How can I show the importance of the topic to others?
■ How might others' feelings differ from my own?

Prewriting helps significantly with this process because it allows you to explore and narrow your thoughts about the topic. By exploring your ideas, you may also discover the pattern of writing that best suits your essay's purpose. Once you have settled on a writing pattern and your opinion about the topic, combine these two elements into one clear sentence that shows your focused topic. The following are examples of generic thesis statements about the topic of hairstyles. They are designed to show how you may state the thesis statement using the different writing patterns you will learn about later in this book.

Illustration:
During the day, I go through several hairstyles.

Cause and Effect:
There are several reasons for wearing a punk hairstyle.
There are several effects of unflattering hairstyles.

Classification:
Based on the activities I do during the day, my hairstyles can be sorted into four different types.

Comparison and Contrast:
> There are several similarities between my two best friends' hairstyles. There are several differences between the 1930s women's hairstyles and today's women hairstyles.

Argument:
> I am against the new bob hairstyle for women.

Description:
> My brother's Mohawk hairstyle is his trademark.

Narration:
> My experience with styling hair taught me the value of self-image.

Definition:
> A person's hairstyle is the way in which self- identity is revealed.

BUILDING SKILLS 2-1: Recognizing Statements of Opinions

Write *OS* next to the sentences that are opinion statements and *FACT* next to those that are factual statements. Remember that an effective thesis statement states an opinion about the topic. It does not state a fact.

1. Hurricanes are storms. _____

2. Art is effective at teaching children how to express their feelings. _____

3. Paris is the capital of France. _____

4. Divorce can have positive effects on children. _____

5. Spring is one season in a calendar year. _____

6. We should adopt stem-cell research because it can save lives. _____

7. Writing proper English is beneficial for job hunting. _____

8. Childhood obesity is a serious problem in the United States. _____

9. The sun is out today. _____

10. Our parents' childhoods were simpler than today's childhoods. _____

You can mention the specific **supporting ideas** of your essay in a thesis, but that is not mandatory. Stating the supporting ideas in the thesis helps you lay out the specific plan for developing the body paragraphs and offers readers a prediction or projection of the supporting ideas. Because of its predictive nature, this sentence in the introduction is called the **forecasting statement** or **plan of development.**

Prewriting helps with the development of the forecasting statement. Through the process of exploring ideas about your topic, you may discover ideas you could use for supporting your focus. To decide on the points you may use in the forecasting statement, ask yourself:

- What kinds of ideas would best explain or support my opinion about the topic?
- What ideas may be relevant as support for my thesis?
- How might I organize these supporting ideas?
- Should I present a list of examples? A story? A comparison? A description? Specific examples? Which ones? A combined method of patterns?

Once you determine the pattern and the supporting ideas you could use for the thesis statement, organize these ideas into a logical order. Then, condense them into brief points, so you can list them. The list of supporting ideas is your forecasting statement. Often, it is combined with the thesis statement, although it may stand alone. Consider the following example:

Topic:	Children
Opinion:	Children bring changes to a marriage
Writing pattern:	Examples of the changes children bring
Supporting ideas:	Family unit
	Couple time /intimacy
	Money

How would you write the thesis with a forecasting statement for this topic? Use the supporting ideas that show the writing pattern and explain the opinion.

Without forecasting statement:

Married couples who have children experience several changes in their lives.

With forecasting statement:

Children bring changes to a married couple's family unit, intimacy, and money.

BUILDING SKILLS 2-2: Recognizing Effective Thesis Statements

Write *TS* next to the sentences that are effective thesis statements and *TOPIC* next to the sentences that are not thesis statements. Remember that an effective thesis statement is a complete sentence that states an opinion about the topic and indicates a pattern of writing.

1. Several steps could be used to deal with the dilemma of child labor. _____

2. Divorce occurs for several reasons. _____

3. Hardships of living with a roommate. _____

4. A career in sports medicine provides several benefits. _____

5. We should adopt stem-cell research because it has important advantages. _____

6. Although my parents have different personalities, they are similar in their expectations of us. _____

7. Texting has become today's standard for communication. _____

8. Religious acceptance. _____

9. Antique collectors can be grouped based on the valuable items they accumulate. _____

10. Stress is pressure that never lets up. _____

BUILDING SKILLS 2-3: Completing a Thesis Statement

Complete the following phrases to make each one a clear thesis statement. A topic and part of the focus or opinion is given, and the missing part may be more than one word.

1. Working with other students in small groups can be _____
_____
_____

2. A lottery win can _____
_____
_____

➡

3. Texting is _____ for the English language.

4. Politicians are _____ for our country.

5. Credit card fraud is _____

_____

_____

BUILDING SKILLS 2-4: Writing Effective Thesis Statements

Prewrite on each of the following topics; then, on the lines below, write a thesis statement for each topic. You may include forecasting statements as part of your thesis statements.

1. Housing

_____

_____

_____

2. Fame

_____

_____

_____

3. Entertainment

_____

_____

_____

4. Greed

_____

_____

_____

5. Humanitarianism

_____

_____

_____

When writing your introduction and thesis statements, follow these suggestions:

- **Avoid announcing, apologizing, or complaining about your writing intentions,** especially in your thesis statement. Do not use sentences that announce your intentions like this:

  In this essay, I will write about the need for performance evaluations.

  My purpose in writing this is to get you to see how unfair the tax proposal is.

  Do not use sentences that apologize about your intentions like this:

  Forgive me if I offend you with my opinion about the death penalty.

  Do not use sentences that complain about your topic like this:

  Even though dating is not my favorite subject to discuss, I will still share with you my feelings about it.

- **Do not state the thesis statement _only_ without introductory sentences.** If the thesis statement is the only sentence in the introduction then you do not have an introduction paragraph but just a statement of opinion. In addition, you will not be able to capture the reader's attention and interest.
- **Avoid writing long introductions.** The length of an introduction varies, but be sure that it only introduces and not develops ideas. Development is reserved for the supporting paragraphs in the body of the essay.

Consider this example of an essay's introductory paragraph with a thesis statement.

They eliminate pain, fight disease, and save lives, yet pre-scription drugs can create painful addictions or be sure killers depending on the user. — *Hook for a dramatic start*

Prescription drugs are easily accessible especially medical painkillers like Valium and Vicodin. While they are medical sensations for almost every kind of ailment imaginable, if used in an abusive manner, painkillers can create a horrific hell for those who abuse them. — *General information about the topic*

Because prescription painkiller drugs lead to several negative repercussions for the abuser, strict laws and regulations ought to be increased to help with this addictive and abusive use of pain medication. — *Thesis statement*

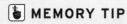

MEMORY TIP

Thesis Statement = Focused Topic (Opinion about Topic + Writing Pattern)

BUILDING SKILLS 2-5: Thesis Statement Language

Read each thesis statement and write *A* next to those that announce, an *AP* next to those that apologize, and *C* next to those that complain.

1. While I am not fond of this subject, there are three problems for users of Twitter. _____

2. I want to share with you that not marrying in your twenties has many benefits. _____

3. I humbly say I like Paris, the capital of France. _____

4. I do like the subject about dogs as guides for the blind. _____

5. To begin with, illegal drug use is a serious problem among our nation's youth. _____

6. It is my humble opinion that traditional marriage is outdated. _____

7. Although I hate dogs, obedience training helps them in several ways. _____

8. In this essay, I will discuss beauty pageants. _____

9. I hope I do not offend my audience with my opinion on stem-cell research. _____

10. What to do during a catastrophe is the subject of this essay. _____

BUILDING SKILLS 2-6: Writing an Introduction

Pick one of the thesis statements that follow and write an introduction paragraph, being sure to include a hook and the thesis statement.

1. The lyrics in current popular music songs affect (or do not affect) the way our youth behave.

_____

_____

_____

_____

_____

_____

_____

_____

_____

_____

_____

_____

2. A recent program or event on my college campus was (or was not) successful.

_____

_____

_____

_____

_____

_____

_____

_____

_____

_____

Body: Supporting Paragraphs

The body of an essay is composed of supporting paragraphs that explain the thesis statement. **Supporting paragraphs** are sometimes called body paragraphs because they make up the main part of the discussion that explains or shows the thesis statement. They must be unified or related to the thesis. They also need coherence so that they flow smoothly and logically. You may use as many supporting paragraphs as you feel you need to explain your thesis statement. Each supporting paragraph includes the following:

1. **Topic sentence:** The topic sentence in an essay is not one of opinion but one that expresses the main idea to be developed in each body or supporting paragraph. It tells the reader what main point will be explained in each body paragraph. Generally, it may be the first sentence for each supporting paragraph; however, it may be placed in the middle or at the end of the supporting paragraph. Topic sentences achieve unity—agreement or harmony—among the ideas to advance or prove the opinion in the thesis.

2. **Development sentences**: These are informational sentences that come after the topic sentence and provide details about the topic. Development sentences help the reader understand your topic sentence. Because development

sentences clarify, explain, or make it easier for readers to remember the main idea in each supporting paragraph, they should contain a variety of information such as facts about the topic sentence, reasons for the topic sentence, examples for the topic sentence, or details to clarify the topic sentence and help the reader accept each important point in your essay.

As the writer, you choose what specific information points to use to explain your topic sentences. Development information comes from many sources and depends on your audience and your purpose for writing. Personal experience, observations, facts, statistics, case studies, or memories can help you make your topic sentences clear and convincing. There is no set length, no prescribed number of lines or sentences for development sentences. They need to be long enough to accomplish their purpose of explaining each topic sentence and short enough to be interesting.

 MEMORY TIP

An easy way to remember the types of development sentences is with an acronym: FRIEDs, a term coined by Dr. Karen Russikoff.

F = **F**acts

R = **R**easons

I = **I**ncidents

E = **E**xamples

D = **D**etails

s = for plural use of facts, reasons, incidents, examples, and details

This acronym is used in this book as an optional way to refer to development sentences.

Do not stick to one kind of development sentence. Sometimes, a writer may provide only facts for each supporting paragraph. Stringing facts together limits the writing and bores readers. Since your writing needs to engage readers, it is important to provide a variety of development sentences to keep your supporting paragraph interesting, thoughtful, and coherent. Keep in mind that one sentence can have several pieces of information (or FRIEDs) in it.

Detail *Reason and example*
↓ ↓
The look of the truck is | masculine and rugged, | and | it can drive over challenging terrain | because it is four-wheel drive.
↑
Reason and fact

See the full example of development sentences (or FRIEDs) in the *Dream Vehicles* essay that follows on page 000.

3. **Transitions**: These are words or expressions used to help the reader keep up with the flow and logic of thoughts. Transitions create coherence in an essay because they show how the supporting paragraphs have been arranged, or ordered. The most common orders are:
   - **time** or **chronological order** (first, second, third...)
   - **spatial order** (in front, next to, behind...)
   - **importance** or **emphatic order** (least to most important)

   In organizing your body paragraphs, it is important to use transitions to move the reader through your sequence of supporting ideas. Transitions also help you indicate the writing pattern you have decided to use. Generally, the pattern of writing you use to develop your thesis statement determines the transitions you use to move through the body paragraph's supporting ideas.

MEMORY TIP

Here are some examples of the most common transitions you may use to help order your body paragraphs.

Transitions showing **time** include:

after	at first	before	during	earlier
eventually	finally	later	next	now
soon	then	today	meanwhile	while

Transitions of **space** include:

above	near	to the right	below
at the back	on top	under	beside
behind	on the bottom	over	between
closer in	next to	inside	in back
in front	to the left	on top	outside

Transitions of **importance** include:

first	especially	moreover	last
second	furthermore	principally	in fact
most important	least of all	however	moreover
above all	most of all	in addition	similarly

4. **Unity and coherence:** These elements are essential for the flow of logic between and within the body paragraphs. They solidify the support for the thesis statement and help create a logical, clear, and organized essay.

   ■ Unity means agreement. In essay writing, agreement comes in the form of supporting paragraphs that present and explain ideas that relate directly to the thesis statement. Select and communicate supporting ideas that do not stray from the focus in your topic sentence. Most importantly, uniting or linking the supporting paragraphs to the thesis statement increases your credibility or believability as a writer. Every sentence in the body of the essay must support the opinion stated in the thesis statement.

   ■ Coherence means consistent or clear. In essay writing, consistency and clarity help the writer's ideas flow smoothly and logically. Coherence requires that the supporting paragraphs are organized in a sequential manner to move the reader from one supporting paragraph to another or from idea to idea within each paragraph. To achieve coherence within and between supporting paragraphs, transitional words or expressions/phrases are essential. Transitional words like *first, then, last* guide the reader from one idea to the next. Refer to Appendix B for a full list of transitions.

BUILDING SKILLS 2-7: Supporting Paragraphs and Thesis Statements

Develop a thesis statement based on the list of supporting sentences provided.

1. a. The sound system from my home television is mediocre compared to the theater surround sound system.
   b. The huge high-definition screen offers a better picture than the screen on my home television.
   c. The concession stands offer more choices for food than what I have at home.
   d. I have to clean my own mess at home.

   Thesis statement:

   _____

   _____

   _____

2. a. Driving behind slow drivers can cause road rage.
   b. Driving behind cars with no brake lights can cause drivers anxiety.
   c. Tailgating can cause drivers to become angry.

Thesis statement:

_____

_____

_____

BUILDING SKILLS 2-8: Writing Supporting Sentences

For each thesis statement, write three supporting topic sentences as the basis for supporting paragraphs.

1. Thesis: Homeowners need to consider several things when buying a new house.

   Support 1:

   _____

   _____

   Support 2:

   _____

   _____

   Support 3:

   _____

   _____

2. Thesis: Playing a sport teaches a person several valuable skills.

   Support 1:

   _____

   _____

   Support 2:

   _____

   _____

   Support 3:

   _____

   _____

BUILDING SKILLS 2-9: Writing Supporting Paragraphs

Select one of the introductions you wrote for Building Exercise 2-6 and write a supporting paragraph that explains your thesis statement. You could write more than one supporting paragraph; however, be sure to develop fully your idea(s).

Topic and Introduction Chosen:

_____

_____

_____

Supporting Paragraph:

_____

_____

_____

_____

_____

_____

_____

_____

_____

_____

_____

_____

_____

_____

Conclusion Paragraph

The conclusion paragraph is the last paragraph in the essay designed to bring the discussion to a satisfying close. It is your last chance to persuade readers of your point of view or to impress yourself upon them as a writer and thinker. It should give the reader the feeling that you have said all you want to say about your topic. Its function is primarily to establish a sense of closure. When you start a conclusion, consider using any or all of the following methods:

- Restate the thesis statement in different words.
- Make a final observation about the focused topic and/or supporting paragraphs.
- Offer a thoughtful remark about the topic.
- Summarize the supporting paragraphs in the body of your essay.

> 🖐 **MEMORY TIP**
>
> Consider this acronym to remember the methods for concluding an essay:
> **RORS.**
>
> **R**estating
>
> **O**bserving
>
> **R**emarking
>
> **S**ummarizing

At the end of the conclusion, you want to leave your readers with a memorable impression about your topic and thesis statement. The impression you create will shape the impression that stays with readers after they have finished reading the essay. There are several ways to create memorable impressions:

■ **A prediction**

In the next ten years, we will continue to hear about new bad driving laws.

■ **Quotation**

As observed by Gilbert Parker, "Nothing is so unproductive as the law. It is expensive whether you win or lose."

■ **Recommendation/suggestion**

Drivers should be appreciative of the new driving laws as they help protect their safety and the safety of others on the road.

We should appreciate our country for providing us with laws that increase our driving safety.

■ **A call to action—the reader should do something**

Go to recycle facilities and be a part of the team that stands against environment abuse.

You should avoid the following in your conclusion:

■ **Announcing your conclusion.** Do not use sentences that announce you are closing your discussion; then readers will not bother to read your conclusion because you are telling them instead of showing them. Avoid sentences like:

I would like to conclude this discussion with this statement: We should repeal the laws.

I want to end with this thought…

■ **Complaining or apologizing about the assignment.** Do not include sentences about your view of the essay assignment like:

> Well, this is my humble opinion on the matter, and I am sorry if I have confused you with my thoughts.

> Although this is not my favorite subject to discuss, I told you how I feel about it.

■ **Presenting an afterthought or new idea.** Do not add something you forgot to discuss in the body of the paper. That leaves the reader feeling unsatisfied with your discussion.

Consider this example of a conclusion paragraph.

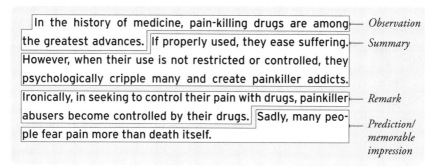

In the history of medicine, pain-killing drugs are among the greatest advances. — *Observation*

If properly used, they ease suffering. — *Summary*

However, when their use is not restricted or controlled, they psychologically cripple many and create painkiller addicts.

Ironically, in seeking to control their pain with drugs, painkiller abusers become controlled by their drugs. — *Remark*

Sadly, many people fear pain more than death itself. — *Prediction/ memorable impression*

Title

You should select your essay's title after you have written a rough draft. The title should be:

■ **Reflective of your overall discussion.** A title should come from the supporting or development sentences.

■ **Catchy, original, and short—no more than a few words.** You may use nonstandard English words so long as your language is respectful. Make your titles as catchy as possible to "hook" the reader or to compel and to excite the reader to read your essay.

Examples of bland titles:

> Examples of Greed
> The Contrast between Mexico and America

Examples of engaging titles:

> Common Cents
> Going to Extremes

■ **Capitalized.** Capitalize all major content words in the title. Generally, articles such as *the, a, an,* and prepositions such as *to, of, from, by, on, in, with, for* are not capitalized if they are not the first words in the title.

Love in the Nick of Time

 MEMORY TIP

In your titles, avoid using:

■ Periods at the end, underlining, or quotation marks.

■ The name of the assignment as the title, for example: The Examples Paragraph

EXAMPLE OF AN ESSAY

Dream Vehicles

For as long as I can remember, cars have fascinated me. By the age of sixteen, I understood how to assemble a car from scratch. Over the years, I have learned the strengths and weaknesses of many vehicles, and I've dreamt of owning certain ones. While I love all kinds of vehicles, I have three favorite ones that I plan on owning someday.

The first vehicle I'd love to own is a Chevy Silverado truck. A utilitarian vehicle can carry heavy loads and withstand rough treatment. The look of the truck is masculine and rugged, and it can drive over challenging terrain because it is four-wheel drive. Since I love camping, it would be an ideal vehicle to hold my camping gear and to fit all my friends. Moreover, it has a good safety record in accidents.

A second vehicle I'd like to own is the Jaguar XF. It has a unique body style that is sleek, modern, yet family-friendly. It is a four-door sedan with plush seats and a big trunk. It has over 300 horse power, yet the gas mileage it gets makes it a worthy commuter car. It is manufactured in Britain where a superior method of mechanical engineering is used.

The least needed but most desired vehicle I'd love to own is a Porsche Carrera 4S. It has over 340 horse power and weighs very little, so it is one of the fastest cars ever produced. Since the first Porsche was introduced in 1948 (fact), the German engineering has continued to put it at the forefront of both racing and street cars. The Carrera body style is distinctive in its curvaceous lines and low aerodynamics. It is a two-door, sleek bullet that can reach 175 miles per hour. It is my ultimate dream car and the reason for my savings account.

A Chevy Silverado truck, a Jaguar XF, and a Porsche Carrera 4S are the vehicles I'd like to own. Among all the other vehicles, those three dream vehicles meet all my driving and pleasure needs.

◖ BUILDING SKILLS TOGETHER 2-1: Evaluating the Parts of an Essay

Working with a partner, read this essay and, on a separate sheet of paper, answer the evaluation questions that follow.

Working for College.doc

Working for College

My parents cannot pay for my education, so I have to rely on working and making enough money to cover my college tuition and other expenses. I have held different jobs over the last 3 years, but for the last year I have been working as a waiter at a local restaurant. Sadly, working as a waiter at Bellagio's is the worst job I have ever had.

First, the work schedule is exhausting. Every day except Monday, I work from two in the afternoon until eleven at night. My work consists of greeting customers, serving them food and beverages, and ushering them out of the restaurant, all while smiling cheerfully. I am on my feet for nine hours and some days I am so tired that I have to remind myself to paste a smile on my face. When I get home at midnight, I collapse into my bed until the alarm clock blasts me awake at 6 in the morning. I get up and study for a few hours before I head out for my morning classes.

Second, the customers are dirty and sometimes hard to clean up after. I have observed that when people go out to eat, they are extra messy because they know someone else has to clean up. After they are ushered out the door, I have to go back and pick up the dirty napkins from the floor, wipe the bread and food crumbs from the tables and chairs, and gather and take the dirty plates and cutlery to the kitchen. Sometimes I even have to mop up sticky sauce or plastered foods that have been dropped on the floor and stepped on.

Often, I have thought of quitting, but the long hours and messy customers have taught me that I do not want to be a waiter for all my life, so I am sticking with this job for as long as it pays the college tuition. My college degree will bring me better opportunities.

1. Consider the introduction. What method is used to "hook" the reader's interest? Does the introduction offer sufficient introductory sentences about the topic?

_____

_____

_____

_____

2. Underline the thesis statement. What is the focused topic or opinion? Is the thesis statement effective? What might you change or add?

_____

_____

_____

_____

3. How many supporting paragraphs are used to develop the thesis? What order are they in?

_____

_____

4. Do the supporting paragraphs provide strong support or explanation of the thesis statement? Why or why not?

_____

_____

5. Consider the development sentences (or FRIEDs) in each supporting paragraph. How many and which ones are used in each paragraph? Are they effective? Explain your answer.

_____

_____

_____

_____

_____

_____

_____

_____

_____

_____

6. Circle the transition words or expressions. Are they effective in moving you through the supporting paragraphs? List them and determine the order they show.

_____

_____

_____

7. Is there a conclusion paragraph? How does it end the essay's discussion? What method(s) (restating, observing, remarking, summarizing) is used to conclude? Explain your answer.

_____

_____

_____

8. What point of view is used in the essay? Is it relevant to the writer's purpose? Is it consistent throughout the essay?

_____

_____

9. Is the title effective? Why or why not?

_____

_____

BUILDING SKILLS 2-9: Creating Outlines for Essays

Select one of the thesis statements you developed in Building Skills 2-4 or Building Skills 2-7. On a separate sheet of paper, use that thesis statement to compose a formal or informal outline for an essay. Refer to Chapter One for a thorough explanation on outlines.

❚ BUILDING SKILLS TOGETHER 2-2: Writing an Essay

Use the prewriting you did for the Building Skills Together 1-1 on page 20 to write a structured essay about social networking sites. Make sure you include all of the following parts in your essay.

1. Introduction and Thesis Statement:

2. Supporting Paragraph 1: _____
    Development Sentences (or FRIEDs): _____

3. Supporting Paragraph 2: _____
    Development Sentences (or FRIEDs): _____

4. Supporting Paragraph 3: _____
    Development Sentences (or FRIEDs): _____

Conclusion Paragraph: _____
_____
_____
_____

CHAPTER THREE: Rewriting Essays

In Chapters One and Two, you learned about the prewriting and writing steps. Now, you will learn about the third and last step in the writing process: rewriting. Once you have a rough draft, you can begin the third stage of the writing process. The rewriting step helps you improve your rough draft so that your communication is logical and effective. Rewriting helps polish your essay, so it is free of structural and grammatical errors.

WHY REWRITE?

Rewriting is critical to good writing since the rough draft is never a perfect one. Before you rewrite, take a break from your rough draft for a while to distance yourself from your ideas and words in order to have the ability to evaluate them objectively in the rewriting process. Rewriting involves two stages: revising and editing. Revising and editing should not be done at the same time as they are considered different parts of the writing process. **Revising** is concerned with the ideas and the structure (introduction, thesis statement, supporting paragraphs, development sentences, and conclusion) of your essay whereas **editing** is concerned with the grammar or structure of sentences (like verb tenses, fragments, run-ons, comma splices, punctuation, spelling, etc.). Therefore, to be a more efficient writer, do the revising before the editing so that you are cleaning up the bigger writing problems before the smaller writing problems.

Note: In some college classes, you may be asked to participate in peer feedback workshops where you exchange drafts with others to get revision and editing input. Chapters Four through Twelve offer peer feedback suggestions for each pattern of writing.

Revising

Revision means to "see again." You need to "see again" your rough draft to determine if your structure, including ideas, development, and organization, is convincing and correct. During revision, you are looking at the flow of your ideas. Specifically, you are looking at the elements of your essay: the introduction and thesis statement, the supporting paragraphs, the development sentences, and the conclusion paragraph. That is, did your ideas convey what you meant to say? In "seeing" your rough draft again, you may find that you have to change the structure, order, or content of all or some of your paragraphs. Read your draft aloud and mark it as you go, so you can come back and add, cut, or change certain parts. Consider these effective revision strategies:

- ☐ **Set aside your essay and let it cool for a while.** Take a walk, watch a show, have dinner, listen to music, or talk to friends before you try revising your newly completed rough draft. Immediately after writing, your ideas are still too fresh, and your revision effort will be ineffective.

- ☐ **Print a draft if you have it typed on a computer.** Printing a draft allows you to "see" your work laid out in front of you, so you can write comments, underline, or cross out sentences or parts.

- ☐ **Review the assignment and your prewriting notes.** Before looking at your draft, reread the instructor's guidelines, your prewriting ideas, and the model for the pattern of writing you are using.

- ☐ **Read your essay aloud with a "critical eye."** Consider the elements that make your essay clear and strong and the elements that weaken your essay. Closely examine the structure of the essay. Look to see if you have the following:

  - ☐ **Introduction Paragraph:** The introduction "hooks" the reader, gives enough specific remarks about the topic, and provides a clear and focused thesis statement.

  - ☐ **Thesis Statement:** The main idea is clearly stated and contains an opinion and an indication of writing pattern.

  - ☐ **Supporting Paragraphs:** Several supporting ideas are included to explain, show, or justify the thesis.

  - ☐ **Development Sentences:** Specific information sentences explain each supporting paragraph.

  - ☐ **Unity:** All supporting paragraphs and development sentences in the body of the essay relate to the thesis.

  - ☐ **Coherence:** Supporting paragraphs and development sentences flow logically and smoothly through the use of transitions. (See Appendix B.)

  - ☐ **Conclusion Paragraph:** The conclusion ends the essay by restating the thesis statement, summarizing supporting paragraphs, and/or offering thoughtful observations or remarks.

☐ **Point of View:** The point of view—first (*I, we*), second (*you*), or third person (*he, she, it*)—is relevant to the purpose of the essay and is used consistently.

☐ **Title:** The title is appropriate and catchy for the essay's topic and discussion.

☐ **Rewrite the parts that need changing.** Whatever elements are weak, write suggestions to make them stronger; you may want to consult your prewriting again to see what ideas you could add or change.

Unity in Essays

It is your responsibility as the writer to show or explain your opinion to the readers. Therefore, provide logical and clear support that justifies or validates your view on the topic. In addition, supporting paragraphs must relate directly to the thesis statement, so the essay has **unity** or consistency. That means, in your supporting paragraphs, you should concentrate on explaining the focused topic you have provided. Therefore, select and communicate topic sentences that connect to or agree with the opinion in your thesis statement. Most importantly, uniting or linking the topic sentences to the thesis statement increases your credibility or believability as a writer.

For example, if your essay's thesis is about the harmful disadvantages of electronic communication devices like cell phones and smartphones on good communication, offer united supporting ideas in your topic sentences that show or discuss some of these disadvantages. If, in that same essay, you discuss the companies that created the various brands of cell phones like Blackberrys or iPhones, you would not produce an essay with unity because those topics do not relate to the focused topic of disadvantages of electronic communication devices. Instead, they relate to the creators of electronic devices you would buy or recognize. For a united essay on this topic, you may offer the following topic sentences for your supporting paragraphs:

Electronic communication devices make it hard to meet or socialize face-to-face with people.

Electronic communication devices trivialize relationships.

Electronic communication devices are major distractions.

 BUILDING TIP

Prewriting techniques such as listing, clustering, or outlining help you find and link appropriate supporting sentences for stronger paragraph unity.

Coherence in Essays

The supporting paragraphs are organized in a sequential manner to move the reader from one idea to the next. That means they have to be put in a logical order, so they will be easy for your readers to follow and provide **coherence** or clarity to your ideas. You create coherence when you arrange the supporting paragraphs in an order sequence of *time, importance,* or *space.* You indicate the sequence of the supporting paragraphs when you use **transitions**—words like *first, then, last*—to guide the reader from one paragraph to the next.

For example, for a thesis about the disadvantages of electronic communication devices like cell phones and smart phones on good communication, you could use transitions of importance for the supporting sentences. Consider the following outline of a united and coherent essay on harmful disadvantages of electronic communication devices like cell phones and smartphones:

Thesis statement:
> **Electronic communication devices like cell phones and smartphones have harmful disadvantages to good communication.**

Supporting paragraph 1:
> **The first disadvantage is the hardship in meeting and socializing face-to-face with people.**

Supporting paragraph 2:
> **The second disadvantage is that electronic communication devices trivialize important relationships.**

Supporting paragraph 3:
> **The most important disadvantage is that electronic communication devices are a major source of distraction.**

👆 MEMORY TIP

Unity and coherence are two critical elements essential for sustaining the required elements in an essay. When revising, pay close attention to your supporting paragraphs and transitions.

- **Unity** is about using **supporting paragraphs** that relate directly to the thesis statement.

- **Coherence** is about using **transitions** between the supporting paragraphs to move the readers logically and smoothly through the essay.

BUILDING SKILLS 3-1: Revising for Unity and Coherence in Essays

Unity in an essay means that all supporting paragraphs are directly related to the thesis statement. Read this essay and answer the questions that follow.

Barbie Doll Syndrome

Barbie is a fashion doll that was launched in the 1950s. Its creator, Ruth Handler, based her idea for the doll on her daughter's preoccupation with paper dolls and her imitation of adult roles. The adult-bodied doll was named Barbie after Handler's daughter's nickname. For decades, Barbie has been a cultural icon and an important part of the doll market; however, it has also been the topic of many controversies and lawsuits about the doll's lifestyle. The criticisms against her are warranted because children regard this doll as a role model and attempt to imitate her unrealistic body image. This "Barbie doll syndrome" has several dangerous effects on young females.

One of the most common consequences of trying to attain Barbie's body image is anorexia, a serious eating disorder. Barbie's radical proportions inspire young females to believe that girls should have tiny waists, long legs, big breasts, and blonde hair to be acceptable to males. No matter the age, many females will try to attain that Barbie-like body through dieting and exercising. Often, the notion of dieting leads to the practice of anorexia, which is characterized by extreme low body weight with an obsessive fear of gaining weight. Individuals with anorexia control body weight through voluntary starvation, diet pills and diuretic drugs, or excessive exercise. Anorexia is addicting and may lead to death.

Another effect is plastic surgery. For some females, dieting and exercising is not enough to get them to that Barbie-like body, so they turn to plastic surgery. Some females turn to plastic surgery to correct a physical defect or to alter a part of the body they are not happy about. The most commonly performed plastic surgeries on young females include breast augmentations, nose shaping, liposuction, and facelifts. The risks involved in plastic surgery depend on the procedure being performed; however, there are many cases of malpractice and of adverse side effects from certain procedures.

The most troubling effect is suicide. Children have always innately associated themselves with their toys to give them information about their own identities. This allows them to form and develop their self-image at an early age. When they play with Barbie, young girls project their self-image onto the doll in an attempt to identify with it. This sense of identity stays with them through their adolescence and into their adulthood. When dieting and plastic surgery are not enough to make young females' sense of identity better, many seek suicide as a means to end the personal and social pain they experience from falling short of the ideal image.

Anorexia, plastic surgery, and suicide are several effects of the Barbie doll syndrome. Barbie may be a mere doll, but in the hands of little girls this doll may be a ticking bomb because it incites many of them to reshape themselves, sometimes in severely tragic ways.

1. Consider the introduction. What method of "hooking" the reader's interest is used? What is the thesis statement?

_____

_____

_____

2. What are the topic sentences of each supporting paragraph that unify this essay? Are there sentences that do not relate to the thesis statement? If so, list them.

_____

_____

_____

_____

3. Underline the transition words in the essay. Are they sufficient? Where might you add transitions to add to the coherence of the essay?

_____

_____

Editing

Editing means proofreading and includes making changes in the grammar of your writing. At this point, you look for sentence errors in: spelling, punctuation, conjunction use, pronoun use, and word choice. If some sentences cannot be easily understood when you read them aloud, edit them. When you edit, you are looking at the sentence-level for how your words or sentences are used. Here are some effective editing strategies:

☐ **Read your paper aloud.** Listen carefully to your words and sentences. You can hear and see missing words, misspelled words, repetitive phrases, and incorrect constructions.

☐ **Use spell check, grammar check, and the dictionary tool.** All word-processing programs include spell check, grammar check, and dictionary options. Spell check is helpful in detecting misspelled words, but pay attention to how you've written the words because computer programs miss words like *form* and *from* or *their* and *there*. Because spell check does not catch every error you should still proofread your writing carefully. The grammar check option helps you with sentence-construction errors including verb tense, fragments, run-ons, parallel structure, apostrophe use, passive voice, and capitalization. The dictionary option helps you find the most appropriate words to use since it gives you synonyms, antonyms, and/or definitions of words. Do not assume what words mean; always look up any words you are uncertain of because using the right words makes a powerful impression on your readers. Use the thesaurus tool carefully. It provides suggestions for alternate words that mean the same thing, but do not replace a word unless you understand its meaning and know it is the right word to explain or describe your thoughts.

☐ **Examine your sentences.** Using Appendix A, study your individual sentences to see if you have correctly punctuated coordinating or subordinating conjunctions. Also, be sure that you have used a variety of sentences.

☐ **Use spelling, diction, and sentence construction questions to edit your work.**

Spelling and Diction

☐ Are appropriate and specific words used?

☐ Are slang words/phrases, text message language, or clichés used?

☐ Are words spelled correctly?

☐ Are words capitalized correctly?

Sentence Construction

☐ Are sentences punctuated correctly—no fragments, run-ons, or comma splices? (See Appendix A.)

☐ Do subjects and verbs agree?

☐ Are the verb tenses consistent?

☐ Are pronouns used correctly? Is point of view consistent?

☐ Are sentences varied in structure? (Check that not only simple sentences are used.)

☐ Are ideas coordinated or subordinated correctly?

In your essays, it is important to <u>avoid</u> the following:

- Writing in second person (using the pronoun *you* or *your*). Most academic writing requires the use of third-person perspective (using the pronouns *she, he, it, they, him, her, them*) and sometimes first-person perspective (using the pronoun *I* or *we*).

- Slang words or phrases such as *chick* (for female), *dude* or *guy* (for male), *sick* (for awesome), *my bad* (for my mistake).

- Text message language such as *LOL* (laugh out loud), *BTW* (by the way), *FYI* (for your information).

- Cliché words or phrases that are figures of speech, euphemisms, or common sayings. Examples include:

always there for me	driving me crazy
got my back	filthy rich
old as dirt or over the hill	raining cats and dogs
fit to be tied	call it a day

👆 **MEMORY TIP**

- **Revision** is concerned with the **idea-level** of the essay = thesis statement, introduction paragraph, supporting paragraphs, development sentences, conclusion paragraph, coherence, and unity.

- **Editing** is concerned with the **sentence-level** or the grammar of the essay = spelling, diction or word choice, and sentence construction.

BUILDING SKILLS 3-2: Editing

Read the following excerpt paragraph and underline the errors you find. Correctly rewrite the paragraph on the lines provided.

People now in days seem to have a cell phone semi-permanently attached to one ear people talk on their cell phones in restaurants in cars even while crossing the street. It is a form of communication that has taken over every facet of our everyday lifes many can't get through the day without their cellphone as they are texting or emailing friends and loved ones throughout the day using their little handy phones. Also, there is no more privacy since they can no longer say that we didn't receive their text or call. Many companies give the user features or indicators to tell them if the message was successful or not. Short of saying there phone was off there is literally no excuse for not answering a phone. So, we are always chatting or texting on cell phones, but are we really socially interacting? Cell phone use is increasing anti-social skills as more people engrossed in their phone conversations instead of there non-phone communications.

_____

_____

_____

_____

_____

_____

_____

_____

_____

_____

_____

_____

_____

_____

_____

_____

_____

_____

_____

_____

PREPARING YOUR FINAL ESSAY FOR SUBMISSION

When you have revised and edited your essay, it is time to produce a clean copy, which means you have to *rewrite* certain parts of your essay to make all the necessary changes and adjustments you discovered during the revision and editing stages. Follow the submission guidelines provided by your instructor, but consider this generic checklist for manuscript submission according to the Modern Language Association (MLA) guidelines:

- Use only 8.5-by-11-inch paper (not torn out of a spiral-bound notebook).
- Print on one side of the paper only.
- Double-space your essay and do not add extra space above or below the title of the paper or between paragraphs. Use Times New Roman font with a 12-point type size.
- Leave one-inch margins all around from the edge of the paper. Left align the text.
- Center the title at the top of the page. Do not underline, italicize, or put quotation marks around the title.
- Put your name, your instructor's name, course title, and date on separate lines against the left margin of the first page of your paper.
- Indent the first line of each paragraph one-half inch or five spaces from the left (hit the *tab* button once).
- Leave one space after each period and one space after each comma.
- Put the page number preceded by your last name in the upper-right corner as the header of each page one-half inch below the top edge. Use Arabic numerals (1, 2, 3. . .)
- Make a copy of your paper or save it on a storage memory device before you submit it, in case of loss.
- Staple together the peer revision worksheets, your rough drafts, and your final draft, if your instructor requires you to do so.

 BUILDING TIP

MLA requirements may change, so be sure to reference the most recent MLA guidelines by visiting www.mla.org.

⬤ BUILDING SKILLS TOGETHER 3-1: Revising
▮ and Rewriting

Work with a partner or small group on the essay you wrote for Building Skills Together 2-2 on page 51 or any essay your instructor has asked you to write. Revise the essay you have written by answering the following questions:

Revising: Idea-level

1. Does the introduction capture the attention of the reader? Are there sufficient specific introductory sentences before the thesis statement? What changes might you make?

2. Underline the thesis. Does it include a focused opinion on the topic and an indication of the writing pattern? What changes might you make?

3. How many supporting paragraphs are used? Are they organized logically with clear topic sentences?

4. Is each supporting paragraph sufficiently developed with enough development sentences (or FRIEDs)? What might you change?

5. Are there clear transition words to move you through the body paragraphs? Where might you make changes?

6. Does the conclusion end the discussion? What method(s) (restating, observing, remarking, summarizing) is used to conclude? How effective is the conclusion? What changes might you make?

7. What is the point of view—first (*I, we*), second (*you*), or third person (*he, she, it*)? Is it relevant to the purpose of the essay? Is it used consistently throughout the essay?

8. Is the title catchy? What changes might you make?

Editing: Sentence-level
Spelling and Diction

1. Are appropriate and specific words used?

2. Are slang words, text message language, or clichés used?

3. Are words spelled correctly?

4. Are words capitalized correctly?

➡

Sentence Construction and Sentence Variety

1. Are sentences punctuated correctly—no fragments, run-ons, or comma splices? (See Appendix A.)

2. Do subjects and verbs agree?

3. Are verb tenses consistent?

4. Are pronouns used correctly? Is point of view consistent?

5. Are sentences varied in structure?

6. Are ideas coordinated or subordinated correctly?

▌ BUILDING SKILLS TOGETHER 3-2: The Three Stages of Writing

Work with a partner on using the three stages of writing. Write a coherent and unified essay and be sure to turn in to your instructor your prewriting activities, your rough draft(s), and your final revised draft. Use the revision questions shown in Building Skills Together 3-1. Choose one of the following topics for your essay:

- The many uses of texting

- The green movement

- Television stereotypes

UNIT TWO: Building Tightly Structured Essays

NOW THAT YOU have learned how to approach the building or writing process, you are ready to create essays. Essay writing requires that you know and use various writing patterns. Some writing patterns follow a prescribed and formal structure, especially when it comes to the thesis statement, the supporting paragraphs, and the conclusion paragraph. The patterns of writing that lend themselves to strict structures are:

- Illustration
- Cause or Effect
- Analysis by Division
- Comparison or Contrast

CHAPTER FOUR: Illustration
Building Essays with Examples

What do you mean when you tell a friend that a diet is *good* or that a show is *bad*? Or that the new nutritional guidelines do not seem helpful to society? To explain such statements, you may **illustrate** or give examples to clarify what you mean. Some college assignments may require that you illustrate your opinion on certain subjects.

Illustration or **exemplification** is the use of several specific examples to explain, clarify, or show the main point or thesis statement. Giving examples is an effective way of explaining or showing concepts to make complex and abstract ideas easier to understand. For example, if you are trying to show what things distract you while driving, you might cite the fact that your cell phone rings every five minutes, your passengers are talking or arguing raucously in the back, and the broken passenger door rattles loudly. In short, illustration gives specific and understandable examples to show the thesis.

WRITING AN ILLUSTRATION ESSAY

Well-chosen examples are essential to this pattern of writing, and you can draw examples from personal experience, observations, or readings. Begin your writing with some prewriting activities that help you reflect on examples for your subject. As you are prewriting, make sure that your examples are:

- specific
- clearly and directly related to the subject
- interesting and believable for the reader

Consider the subject of *hobbies* as a topic. In your prewriting, consider as many hobbies as you know. Listing is a useful approach for illustration. Consider this example.

- Reading
- Dumpster diving
- Swimming
- Tricking out cars
- Astrology charts
- Graffiti
- Contest mania
- Playing the drums
- Cookie decorating

Along the way, you may realize that you are listing some hobbies you actually do and others you may have heard about. Now look at the list again and draw out the examples that may interest you. You may be interested in hobbies you have heard about but do not do yourself, such as *dumpster diving, contest mania, tricking out cars,* or *astrology charts.* Consider these examples carefully. What common focus might they have? What interests you about these four hobbies? How did you hear about them? Maybe some of your friends or relatives actually do these hobbies. This kind of thinking helps you narrow the focus on the subject of hobbies. Maybe you find these hobbies unusual, and you are curious about how they are actually done; then, you may use *unusual hobbies* as a topic. But what about these unusual hobbies? Maybe some of your friends do these hobbies and you would like to understand why they like them. You might narrow this topic further by focusing on the people who do these unusual hobbies: your friends. Now, consider this **focused topic** or opinion about the subject of hobbies: *the unusual hobbies my friends like to do.* Now you have a clear focus and can begin organizing your thoughts into a rough draft.

GENERIC PLAN FOR AN ILLUSTRATION ESSAY

Introduction Paragraph
    Thesis = Focused Topic + Examples
Supporting Paragraph 1: Example 1
    Development Sentences (or FRIEDs)
Supporting Paragraph 2: Example 2
    Development Sentences (or FRIEDs)
Supporting Paragraph 3: Example 3 (most important)
    Development Sentences (or FRIEDs)
Conclusion Paragraph

Introduction Paragraph

The introduction paragraph in an illustration essay should give the reader background information about the topic being focused on in the essay while engaging the reader's interest. Refer to Chapter Two for a complete list of ways to write an introduction paragraph. You may consider providing a definition for or general statements about the topic you are illustrating. Remember to keep the introduction short and relevant to your focused topic.

Thesis Statement

The thesis is the sentence in your introduction that contains your focused topic. In illustration, your focused topic is explained through several specific, well-chosen examples, so your thesis alerts the reader that in your essay, you, the writer, will share several examples that will show your focused topic.

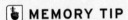

👆 MEMORY TIP

Thesis Statement = Focused Topic + Examples

My friends like to be involved in <u>several kinds</u> of <u>unusual hobbies</u>.
                                 ↑   ↑
                      Examples   *Focused Topic*

While there are many hobbies to participate in, my friends like to engage in <u>three</u> <u>unusual hobbies</u>.
 ↑   ↑
Examples *Focused Topic*

You should phrase the thesis in your own style of writing but be sure to remember that the thesis sentence indicates to the reader your focused topic and the pattern of writing (in this case illustration or the examples to show your topic). You have to invite the readers to ask this question when they read your thesis sentence: *Like what?* Your supporting ideas show the readers exactly *which ones* you mean.

BUILDING SKILLS 4-1: Recognizing Effective Illustration Thesis Statements

Read each thesis statement and write *TS* next to the ones that are effective illustration thesis statements and *X* next to those that are not.

1. Several kinds of extreme sports have developed in the last twenty years.   _____

2. The kind of image for postage stamps in the United States.   _____

3. When the Probe landed on Mars, several things happened.   _____

4. The gold sculpture was truly superb. _____

5. Role models and athletes for our youth. _____

6. Three techniques can help with disciplining misbehaving
   toddlers. _____

7. An employee at a factory must be punctual. _____

8. Heart disease has several clear symptoms. _____

9. Note taking is a good study strategy for college students. _____

10. The library is located beside the campus gym. _____

Supporting Paragraphs

The supporting paragraphs in an illustration essay are the specific, related, and interesting examples you use to show and to explain the focused topic. In the previous example on hobbies, the supporting or topic sentences could be about the following three examples: dumpster diving, contest mania, and tricking out cars. In illustration, each topic sentence includes an example you have decided to use to explain your focused topic. The topic sentences are discussed or organized in order of importance (least to most or most to least important), so you need to choose the order of your three examples before you begin writing. For example, the examples of unusual hobbies could be ordered by how uncommon they are, with the most unusual as the last example: first, *tricking out or modifying cars*; second, *contest mania*; and most important or most unusual, *dumpster diving*.

TRANSITIONS USED IN ILLUSTRATION ESSAYS

As you move your reader through your essay from one major example to another, use any of the following transition words:

also	for one thing	finally	furthermore
another	for instance	first	moreover
one example	for example	second	in addition
another example	in addition	third	specifically
most important example	last but not least		

Consult Appendix B for a complete list of transitions.

BUILDING SKILLS 4-2: Finding Specific Examples

Add supporting topic sentences to each thesis statement.

1. The Internet offers several strong benefits to college students.

   Topic Sentence 1: _____

   _____

   _____

   _____

   Topic Sentence 2: _____

   _____

   _____

   _____

   Topic Sentence 3: _____

   _____

   _____

   _____

2. Children learn negative behaviors from watching certain television shows.

   Topic Sentence 1: _____

   _____

   _____

   _____

   Topic Sentence 2: _____

   _____

   _____

   _____

   Topic Sentence 3: _____

   _____

   _____

   _____

Development Sentences

Development sentences are informational sentences that provide details and explanations about each topic sentence you have presented in your supporting paragraphs. Development sentences help the reader understand each main example you have chosen to use as support for the thesis statement. As the writer, you choose what specific information to use in explaining each topic sentence. Since the topic sentences for each supporting paragraph in an illustration essay indicate the main example that you have chosen to support your thesis, your main examples will be only as good as the details you use in explaining them. Therefore, your details should be in complete sentences that give clear, sufficient, and specific information about why and how each example relates to the thesis sentence.

Remember that development information comes from many sources and depends on your audience and your purpose for writing. Personal experience, observations, facts, statistics, case studies, memories, and more can help you make your topic sentences clear and convincing. There is no set length, no prescribed number of lines or sentences for development sentences. They need to be long enough to accomplish their purpose of explaining each topic sentence and short enough to be interesting.

For each example, consider using different development sentences or FRIEDs (facts, reasons, incidents, examples, or details). Do not stick with one kind of development sentence as that will limit your writing and bore your reader. Also, do not over- or underdevelop one supporting paragraph more or less than the rest of the supporting paragraphs. Use roughly an equal amount of development sentences for each supporting paragraph.

Consider how the example of tricking out cars is developed using facts, reasons, incidents, examples, and details.

The first unusual hobby is car or truck modifying or tricking out. This hobby involves customizing cars or trucks with flared fenders, spoilers or wings, dark tinted windows, and flashy artwork or paint. — *Details and Examples*

My friend, Eric, likes to redesign cars by buying special kits that add flash. — *Reason and Detail*

He does all the work himself from changing the paint color to adding body graphics and performance tires and rims. — *Detail*

The customized touches he adds to his old Pontiac — *Fact*

make it stand apart from the other Pontiacs. — *Reason*

However, the special body kits he buys can be expensive, — *Detail*

so Eric saves most of the money he makes from his part time job at Pets R Us. — *Fact and Reason*

The hobby of car modifying requires a lot of patience, artistic skill, and money.

Conclusion Paragraph

The objective of the conclusion paragraph is to end the discussion; therefore, the conclusion in an illustration essay should summarize the major examples in the order they were presented, reword the thesis sentence, or offer a thoughtful observation or memorable remark. Do not start a new idea, but close off your discussion. One of the sentences in the conclusion may restate the supporting examples like this:

> Car modifying, contests mania, and dumpster diving are several examples of unusual hobbies my friends have.

🖐 MEMORY TIP

Remember these methods for formulating a conclusion paragraph:

- **R**estating
- **O**bserving
- **R**emarking
- **S**ummarizing

You can easily remember these methods by using the acronym RORS.

A conclusion paragraph about hobbies could look like this:

> My friends like to participate in very uncommon hobbies like car modifying, contests mania, and dumpster diving. While they invest a lot of money, time, and effort in their hobbies, they do them for fun and profit. My hobby of reading murder mysteries may seem common by comparison, but I like books and do it for fun.

EXAMPLE OF AN ILLUSTRATION ESSAY

Unusual Hobby Mania

How might people fill up their time when they *have* the luxury of free time? Often, I wonder what hobbies I could participate in if I had more free time. For now, I have *only* one hobby: reading murder mysteries. I try to read as often as I can because it relaxes my mind, but my friends tell me I should have interests that are more exciting. They urge me to join them in their pastimes, but they engage in three very unusual hobbies.

The first unusual hobby is car *tricking out* or modifying. This hobby involves customizing cars with flared fenders, spoilers or wings, dark-tinted windows, and flashy artwork or paint. My friend, Eric, likes to redesign cars by buying special kits that add flash. He does all the work himself from changing the paint color to adding body graphics and performance tires and rims. The customized touches he adds to his old Pontiac make it stand apart from the other Pontiacs. However, the special body kits he buys can be expensive, so Eric saves most of the money he makes from his part-time job at Pets R Us. The hobby of car modifying requires a lot of patience, artistic skill, and money.

The second unusual hobby is contests mania. This hobby is about entering every possible contest to win prizes. It requires filling out forms, making phone calls, writing short stories, clipping UPC or product codes, or sending in photos or videos of random things. It is all about winning the money, the bike, the vacation trip, the new cake pans, or any other kinds of prizes being given away. My friend, Jason, is always surfing the Internet looking for contests, and he is always busy doing something for a contest he wants to enter. He loves the excitement of winning a prize, and in the past he has won a free, three-day, fully paid round-trip ticket to Las Vegas, a free notebook computer, and a $200 shopping spree. However, this hobby requires a lot of persistence and patience.

The most unusual hobby is dumpster diving. This hobby combines adventure, mystery, and cash-making possibilities. It requires going through the trash or dumpsters, preferably in the rich people's neighborhoods, to search for things that other people have owned that are still useful, recyclable, or valuable. The law in most states says that once in the trash, items are fair game, so dumpster diving is legal. Sometimes, people have to climb into dumpsters, but often they use long poles that allow them to just lean over the dumpsters and pull the items up to them. My friend, Manny, has made good cash selling the following items from his dumpster diving: computer parts or accessories, televisions, vacuum cleaners, power tools, bicycles, kids' toys, and small furniture items. While dumpster diving may be a messy and smelly job, it is like a cash-making Treasure Hunt.

My friends like to participate in very uncommon hobbies like car modifying, contests mania, and dumpster diving. While they invest a lot of money, time, and effort in their hobbies, they do them for fun and profit. My hobby of reading murder mysteries may seem common by comparison, but I, like them, do it for fun.

● BUILDING SKILLS TOGETHER 4-1: Evaluating
■ an Illustration Essay

Working in a small group, read the following essay and answer the evaluation questions that follow.

○ ○ ○   📄 Wake-Up Call.doc

Wake-Up Call

In life, we are shaped and molded by the people we encounter and the situations we experience. Through the obstacles we face, we learn what our strengths and weaknesses are and how to use them to the best advantage. As Aristotle once said, "Knowing yourself is the beginning of all wisdom." I know myself, and I know what shaped me as a person and where I am going in the future. In my life, several important factors have helped me become the person I am today.

The first factor in shaping me is college. When I first started school four years ago, I did not know what I wanted to do with my life, and I had a very low opinion of myself. Then, I took Biology and realized that I am fascinated with the human body. Ever since that semester ended, I have been studying and doing well in all my classes. I have researched what career choices I can have with a degree in Biology, and I like where I am heading. Thanks to that biology class, I have a new purpose in life: to become a neurosurgeon.

The second factor in shaping the person I am today is my relationship with my boyfriend, Charles. In the three years I have known him, he has changed my life in so many ways, and he has pushed me and helped me to be a better person. When I met him, I was into partying and troublemaking. At that point in my life, my happiness came first, and I did not care what anyone else said or wanted. I would do what I wanted regardless of other people's feelings. Through his treatment of me, Charles opened my eyes to respecting others and to wanting to make others happy. He is thoughtful and encouraging, and because he is in my life, I am determined to be a good, productive, and compassionate person.

The most important factor in shaping me is the six months I spent in jail over a misdemeanor offense. I had hit rock bottom when, in response to a dare by my friends, I was caught jumping the fence in a neighbor's backyard with a stolen pair of diamond earrings in my hands. The owner of the earrings tried to hold on to me until the police came, but I wrestled with her and gave her minor cuts on her face and arms. I was sentenced to jail for petty theft, trespassing, and simple assault. The positive aspect to all this is that jail time was wake-up time for me. In jail I experienced what it was like to be denied freedoms and to be treated like a criminal. I had a lot of time to think; I hated what I had become and wanted to change myself and to clean up my act. I have been free of trouble for the last three years, living life cleanly and pursuing my education.

My biology class, my boyfriend, and my jail time have been the important factors in shaping me into the person I am today. Like many people, I have had to fall low to rise above my weaknesses, but I have no regrets, only hope for a better future.

1. Consider the introduction. What method is used to "hook" the reader's interest? Does the introduction offer sufficient introductory sentences about the topic?

   _____
   _____
   _____

2. Underline the thesis statement. What is the focused topic or opinion? Is the thesis statement effective? What might you change or add?

   _____
   _____
   _____

3. How many supporting paragraphs are used to develop the thesis? What order are they in?

4. Do the supporting paragraphs provide strong support or explanation of the thesis statement? Why or why not?

5. Consider the development sentences (or FRIEDs) in each supporting paragraph. How many and which ones are used in each paragraph? Are they effective? Explain your answer.

6. Circle the transition words or expressions. Are they effective in moving you through the supporting paragraphs? What order (time, space, or importance) is used to guide the reader from example to example being used?

7. Is there a conclusion paragraph? How does it end the essay's discussion? What method(s) (restating, observing, remarking, or summarizing) is used to conclude? Explain your answer.

8. What point of view is used in the essay? Is it relevant to the writer's purpose? Is it consistent throughout the essay?

9. Is the title effective? Why or why not?

SUGGESTED TOPICS FOR WRITING ILLUSTRATION ESSAYS

Choose one of the following topics or use one of your own, and then use prewriting techniques to develop your draft for an illustration essay.

Influential music bands	Inspiring qualities in a boss/ coworker(s)
Educational hobbies	Typical responsibilities at your job
Qualities of a healthy relationship	Urban myths
House rules	Smart inventions of the 21st century
Beauty secrets	Cultural traditions

BUILDING SKILLS TOGETHER 4-2: Illustration Essay Feedback Checklist

Once the rough draft for your illustration essay is completed, have a partner read it and answer the following revision and editing questions. You may also use this checklist to revise and edit your own essay.

Revising Essay Structure

☐ Does the introduction capture the attention of the reader? Are there sufficient introductory sentences before the thesis statement? What changes might you make?

☐ Underline the thesis. Does it include an opinion on the topic and an indication of illustration? What changes might you make?

☐ Are clear, specific, and related examples used as supporting paragraphs? What changes might you make?

☐ Is each supporting paragraph sufficiently developed with enough development sentences (or FRIEDs)? Where can you make improvements?

☐ Are clear transition words used to move you through the body paragraphs from example to example? Where might you make changes?

☐ Does the conclusion end the essay's discussion? What concluding method (restating, observing, remarking, or summarizing) is used? What changes might you make?

☐ Is the point of view in the essay consistent and relevant? Are any changes needed?

☐ How effective is the title in capturing the essay's content? Why or why not?

Editing Spelling, Diction, and Sentence Construction

☐ Are there any misspelled words?

☐ Are appropriate and specific words used?

☐ Are any slang words, text message language, or clichés used?

☐ Consider sentence structure and correct any errors with:

    ☐ Fragments, run-ons, and comma splices

    ☐ Misplaced or dangling modifiers

    ☐ Verb tense consistency

    ☐ Pronoun agreement

    ☐ Subject and verb agreement

Refer to Appendix A for a review of grammar concepts.

Final Assessment

☐ What do you like the most about the essay?

☐ What are you unclear about or have difficulty with in the essay?

CHAPTER FIVE: Cause or Effect
Building Essays with Reasons or Results

How can alcohol be bad for you? How dangerous is AIDS? Why is algebra a required college course? How would a new assembly procedure affect factory work? All these questions try to determine the causes or effects of an action or situation, and many college-level writing tasks require that you identify causes or effects for a variety of subjects.

Causes and/or effects are used to explain, show, or analyze a subject. A **cause** is what makes something happen. For example, a cause for pollution is fuel emissions from cars and industrial factories. An **effect** is what happens because of something. For example, an effect of pollution is lung cancer or respiratory allergies.

🖐 MEMORY TIP

Other words for **cause** include *factor, reason, source, root,* and *basis.*

Other words for **effect** include *consequence, result, outcome,* and *product.*

Although you may use both causes *and* effects in your writing, it is best to focus on one or other in an essay because it makes it easier to achieve coherence and unity in your text. In short, a cause or effect essay makes it clear whether causes or effects is the focus of the essay and uses specific, detailed, and real causes or effects as support.

✂ BUILDING TIP

To understand causes, consider the **past** for reasons **why** something happened whereas to understand effects, you consider the **future** for possible **consequences** of an action.

WRITING A CAUSE OR EFFECT ESSAY

In using this pattern, your purpose is to give your readers an analysis of causes for or effects of your subject. In fact, the causes or effects that you explain are the actual supporting paragraphs in your essay, so choose them well. Begin your writing with some prewriting activities that will help you reflect on causes or effects about your subject. One useful prewriting technique for this pattern is listing. As you are prewriting, be sure to draw on causes or effects that fit the following characteristics:

- Causes or effects are real, logical, and believable to the reader.
- Causes or effects are directly related and important to the subject.

When you are writing about causes, be careful that you do not include a cause just because it happened beforehand; sometimes coincidence sways the analysis. For example, the fact that you got a bad grade on your math test does not mean it is the reason why you have a headache. Likewise, use the same caution when writing about effects: do not confuse something that happens after something else with the effect. Your headache is not an effect of receiving a bad grade on the math test.

✂ BUILDING TIP

There is a difference between an actual cause and a **contributing factor**. A cause is a direct and definitive reason for something to happen.

> **A causes B.**
>
> **Depression causes alcohol abuse.**

However, a contributing factor *may* be one of the many reasons for something to happen. When you include contributing factors, you use qualifiers (or restricting words such as *often, at times...*).

> **A *may, might, sometimes,* or *can be* the cause for B.**
>
> **Depression, among many other things, may cause alcohol abuse.**

When you state your causes, be careful how you state them, because the meaning shifts depending on the language or qualifiers you use.

Consider the subject of marriage for a cause or effect essay. In your prewriting, write down your subject; then, on the left side list as many reasons for marriage and on the right side list as many effects of marriage. Then, look at your lists.

Causes Effects
love   financial responsibility
money and security   children and family
children   security
companionship   companionship
arranged by family
citizenship

Which side appeals more to you? Which side are you more comfortable developing? Decide on that first; then, isolate the main reasons you feel are most real, logical, believable, and important in your list. Be sure that in selecting the main reasons you are comfortable presenting and discussing them for the reader. Suppose you picked as your topic causes for marriage; you could consider the following three reasons (you may pick more):

■ love
■ children
■ money

Decide on which cause is the most important; there is no right way to do this. It depends on you, the writer, what you find or consider the most important reason or effect, but for this example, you may order your reasons as follows: money, children, and love. Now, you are ready to start your rough draft.

GENERIC PLAN FOR A CAUSE OR EFFECT ESSAY

Introduction Paragraph
    Thesis = Focused Topic + Causes or Effects
Supporting Paragraph 1: Cause or Effect 1
    Development Sentences (or FRIEDs)
Supporting Paragraph 2: Cause or Effect 2
    Development Sentences (or FRIEDs)
Supporting Paragraph 3: Cause or Effect 3 (Most important cause or effect)
    Development Sentences (or FRIEDs)
Conclusion Paragraph

BUILDING SKILLS 5-1: Listing Causes and Effects

Use the following topics to brainstorm lists of causes and effects. Then, circle three causes or three effects to focus on for the topic.

1. Cosmetic surgery
   Causes   Effects

   _____   _____
   _____   _____
   _____   _____
   _____   _____
   _____   _____
   _____   _____
   _____   _____
   _____   _____

2. Video game playing
   Causes   Effects

   _____   _____
   _____   _____
   _____   _____
   _____   _____
   _____   _____
   _____   _____
   _____   _____
   _____   _____

3. Dropping out of high school
   Causes   Effects

   _____   _____
   _____   _____
   _____   _____
   _____   _____
   _____   _____
   _____   _____
   _____   _____

Introduction Paragraph

The introduction paragraph in a cause-or-effect essay should provide pertinent information about the focused topic while engaging the reader's interest. Refer to Chapter Two for a complete list of ways to write an introduction paragraph. General statements are helpful to show the reader the importance of the topic you have chosen to discuss. Remember to keep the introduction paragraph short but filled with relevant material about the focused topic.

Thesis Statement

The thesis statement in a cause or effect essay clearly states the focused topic and the focus on either causes or effects. You may use words like *reasons, effects, results,* and *factors* in your thesis sentence. Phrase your thesis so that the reader knows you are discussing the causes for or effects of your topic.

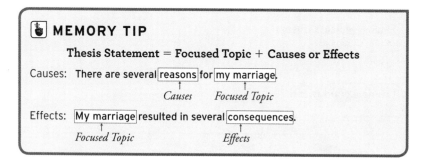

BUILDING SKILLS 5-2: Recognizing Effective Cause or Effect Thesis Statements

Read each sentence and write *TS* next to the ones that are effective cause or effect thesis statements and *X* next to those that are not effective thesis statements.

1. There are several negative effects of spoiling children. _____

2. Increased airport security has created several inconvenient consequences. _____

3. Credit card fraud is on the rise. _____

4. Living at home while going to college has offered several benefits. _____

5. There are several reasons for visiting Alaska. _____

6. Smoking is everywhere nowadays. _____

7. My dream career has always been nursing.   _____

8. I buy fast food for four reasons.   _____

9. For all car drivers, seat belt use offers several important effects.   _____

10. I need to listen to music because, at different times, it helps
    me relax, work, or party.   _____

BUILDING SKILLS 5-3: Writing Cause or Effect Thesis Statements

On a separate sheet of paper, prewrite on each topic; then, write a strong thesis statement for each topic with a clear cause or effect focus.

1. Having plastic surgery

   _____

   _____

2. Losing a good friend

   _____

   _____

3. Peer pressure

   _____

   _____

4. Social networking sites

   _____

   _____

5. Buying a car

   _____

   _____

Supporting Paragraphs

In cause or effect writing, support is made up of the causes or effects chosen to explain the thesis statement. You may choose as many as you want; however, a generally accepted practice is to choose three to five. The three causes of money, children, and love chosen earlier will actually be the topics of the three supporting paragraphs that explain the thesis statement. Supporting paragraphs for cause or effect are organized by order of importance, saving the most important or intense cause or effect for last in order to create a strong impression on the readers. Be sure to use transitions to move the reader from one cause or effect to another.

**TRANSITIONS USED IN CAUSE
OR EFFECT ESSAYS**

Common transitions used in cause or effect essays are:

first cause, second cause, most important cause
one cause, another cause, most important cause
one effect, another effect, most important effect

Consult Appendix B for a complete list of transitions.

Development Sentences

The specific information or the facts, incidents, examples, and details that you use to explain or show each cause or effect must be chosen carefully. Your details need to be in complete sentences that give clear, sufficient, and specific information about why and how each cause or effect relates to the thesis sentence.

Remember that development information comes from many sources and depends on your audience and your purpose for writing. Personal experience, observations, facts, statistics, case studies, memories and more can help you make your topic sentences clear and convincing. There is no set length, no prescribed number of lines or sentences for development sentences. They need to be long enough to accomplish their purpose of explaining each topic sentence and short enough to be interesting. Remember to use roughly an equal amount of development sentences (or FRIEDs) for each cause or effect, so you do not over- or underdevelop your ideas. Development sentences for the supporting idea of money as a cause for marriage may include an example of a famous person who married another for money.

Conclusion Paragraph

The objective of the conclusion paragraph is to use several sentences to end the discussion of the essay. The conclusion, in a cause or effect essay, should not start a new idea. Remember the different concluding methods you can use: restating, observing, remarking, or summarizing (RORS). As part of your concluding sentences, you may combine two of the concluding methods: summarizing the major causes or effects used in the order they were presented, and rewording the thesis statement.

Money, children, and love are three causes for my marriage.

Another way to conclude is to offer some sentences that provide a thoughtful observation or remark about the focused topic.

Money, children, and love are the predominant reasons for getting married. The search for that perfect mate is an ongoing preoccupation, but when that person comes along and the "shoe fits," as it did with Cinderella, one cannot help but be roped into tying the marriage knot.

EXAMPLE OF A CAUSE OR EFFECT ESSAY

Marriage Knot

To tie or not to tie the knot? That is a question of major importance because it involves marrying another person. Marriage is the legal union between two people. Some have a casual view of marriage while others have a serious view of it and regard it as a sacred commitment to be preserved at all costs. While marriage is entered into in different ways, there are several logical reasons for getting married.

One reason is money. People are driven by the need for security, and for many, security means the ability to acquire and retain certain possessions like houses, big bank accounts, or jewelry. In looking to get married, many people look at the potential spouse's ability to afford that security, and that becomes a strong reason to marry that person. For example, the late Anna Nicole Smith married Texas oil business billionaire, who was 63 years her senior. Although she denied marrying him for his money, she battled his family for her share of half of her late husband's $ 1.6 billion estate.

Another reason for getting married is children. Single parenthood is on the rise, and many single parents are looking for potential spouses to help them shoulder the burdens of parenthood. Others seek marriage for the express purpose of reproduction as they want to play that role of provider and nurturer before they are too old to be able to do so, or just because they genuinely want to impart their values and beliefs to their own offspring to pass on their legacies. In fact, women often bring up the "biological clock" issue as a basis for marriage.

The most important reason for getting married is love. Poets and philosophers have tried to pin down the meaning of love, but what it really comes down to is that love means having that someone who cares for you through thick and thin and who will always be by your side to support and cheer you on regardless of the circumstances. Everyone wants to love and be loved. From an early age, fairy tale characters like Cinderella or Rapunzel program people into believing in happily-ever-after endings where the prince carries his princess off into the sunset on his white steed, and they live "happily ever after." They search for that person who will inspire that feeling, and we are trained to believe that the culmination of love is marriage.

Money, children, and love are the predominant reasons for getting married. The search for that perfect mate is an ongoing preoccupation, but when that person comes along, and the "shoe fits" like it did for Cinderella, one cannot help but be roped into tying the marriage knot.

BUILDING SKILLS TOGETHER 5-1: Evaluating a Cause or Effect Essay

Working in a small group, read the following essay and answer the evaluation questions that follow.

The Other.doc

The Other

Up until the age of fourteen, I was a normal teenager, and then all of a sudden I was hit with psoriasis, a skin disease usually marked by red, scaly patches. It started on my forehead during football season, and I was able to control it with over-the-counter treatments. In September of 2005, I started to get psoriasis on my legs and feet, which caused inflammation in my joints and arthritis in my knees and ankles and made walking a painful ordeal. Since then I have not been able to bend my knees and ankles, so I shuffle when I walk. In public several factors make me extremely self-conscious of my appearance.

The first factor in making me feel self-conscious about my appearance is the way people look at me. When people see me, the first thing they ask is, "What's wrong with your head." Sometimes I tell them about my condition, but I am not comfortable doing so. I have heard little kids ask their parents, "What's wrong with that boy?" The parents usually walk away from where I am. I am used to people walking away from me. Usually, my psoriasis is only visible on my forehead because I generally wear pants, but I am saddened to know that in our society having a few blotches on my face will make me a scary person to be avoided at all costs.

The next reason for being self-conscious is how others see my shuffle as a sign of disability. Anybody with arthritis will tell you that it is very painful. For about a year and half, I had a hard time walking. But I learned to walk on my own and do many of the things that someone without my condition could do. My condition is not a disability; I can do all I want to do with my body. In fact, I work in sales, I am always on my feet, and I walk as best as I can because I want to give the customer the best service possible. Many will go to the next associate for help at first because they think I am incapable of doing what they think they need; however, once they are referred to me, they realize that my shuffle does not stop me from giving them what they need.

The most annoying reason for my self-consciousness is that people are always trying to lend me a hand. I am a very independent person albeit with a large, hobbling frame. Many people assume that I need help, so they will try to open doors for me or move out of my way. Usually, I will not take their help because I am not an invalid who is incapable of doing things on his own. In fact, I have had a few people ask me if I have a handicap pass, and I tell them that I do not want one because there are people out there who need those spaces more than I do. I may not be able to walk straight, but I can still walk just like the next person.

The way people look at me, how people see my shuffling, and people lending me a hand are three reasons why I am self-conscious about my physical appearance. Because of my condition, I have become aware that I am viewed as *the other*, pushed away or labeled. While I may have psoriasis as a physical condition, people in our society have it as a mental condition, and it inflames their minds into mistreating those who do not conform to the normal healthy image of a human.

1. Consider the introduction. What method is used to "hook" the reader's interest? Does introduction offer sufficient introductory sentences about the topic?

_____

_____

_____

2. Underline the thesis statement. What is the focused topic or opinion? How effective is it in indicating the cause or effect pattern? What might you change or add?

_____

_____

_____

3. How many supporting paragraphs are used to develop the thesis? What order are they in?

_____

_____

_____

4. Do the supporting paragraphs provide strong support or explanation of the thesis statement? Why or why not?

_____

_____

_____

5. Consider the development sentences (or FRIEDs) in each supporting paragraph. How many and which ones are used in each paragraph? Are they effective? Explain your answer.

_____

_____

_____

6. Circle the transition words or expressions. Are they effective in moving you through the supporting paragraphs? What order (time, space, or importance) is used to guide the reader from one cause or effect to the next? How effective are the transitions?

_____

_____

_____

7. Is there a conclusion paragraph? How does it end the essay's discussion? What method(s) (restating, observing, remarking, or summarizing) is used to conclude? Explain your answer.

_____

_____

_____

8. What point of view is used in the essay? Is it relevant to the writer's purpose? Is it consistent throughout the essay?

_____

_____

_____

9. Is the title effective? Why or why not?

_____

_____

_____

SUGGESTED TOPICS FOR WRITING CAUSE OR EFFECT ESSAYS

Choose one of the following topics or use one of your own and then use prewriting techniques to develop your draft for a cause or effect essay.

Racial profiling	Stereotyping
Pride	Window shopping
Reality television shows	Peer pressure
Glass ceiling	Online shopping
Grades in school/college	Placement tests

◗ BUILDING SKILLS TOGETHER 5-2: Cause or Effect Essay Feedback Checklist

Once the rough draft of your cause or effect essay is completed, have a partner read it and answer the following revision and editing questions. You may also use this checklist to revise and edit your own essay.

Revising Essay Structure

☐ Does the introduction capture the attention of the reader? Are there sufficient introductory sentences before the thesis statement? What changes might you make?

☐ Underline the thesis. Does it include a focused opinion on the topic and an indication of cause or effect? What changes might you make?

☐ Are clear, specific, and related causes (or effects) used as supporting paragraphs? What changes might you make?

☐ Is each supporting cause (or effect) sufficiently developed with enough development sentences (or FRIEDs)? Where can you make improvements?

☐ Are clear transition words used to move you through the body paragraphs from one cause (or effect) to the next cause (or effect)? Where might you make changes?

☐ Does the conclusion end the essay's discussion? What concluding method (restating, observing, remarking, or summarizing) is used? What changes might you make?

☐ Is the point of view in the essay consistent and relevant? Are any changes needed?

☐ How effective is the title in capturing the essay's content? Why or why not?

Editing Spelling, Diction, and Sentence Construction

☐ Are there any misspelled words?

☐ Are appropriate and specific words used?

☐ Are any slang words, text message language, or clichés used?

☐ Consider sentence structure and correct any errors with:

☐ Fragments, run-ons, and comma splices

☐ Misplaced or dangling modifiers

☐ Verb tense consistency

☐ Pronoun agreement

☐ Subject and verb agreement

Refer to Appendix A for a review of grammar concepts.

Final Assessment

☐ What do you like the most about the essay?

☐ What are you unclear about or have difficulty with in the essay?

CHAPTER SIX: Analysis by Division
Building Essays with Parts

As a writing instrument, a wooden pencil can be divided into several functional parts: a wooden barrel, a graphite core or lead, and an eraser. Some college assignments require that you analyze certain subjects by dividing them into their individual parts. Among other courses, biology, chemistry, psychology, and sociology courses commonly require analysis by division essays.

Analysis by division separates a subject into its individual parts to explain how each part works in relation to the subject. The subject must be something that can stand alone such as a pencil, a human body, a company, a hospital, or a book. For example, a desktop computer could be divided into its components so that the reader has a better understanding of what a computer is and how each part contributes to how the computer works as whole.

WRITING AN ANALYSIS BY DIVISION ESSAY

To divide a subject, follow these four steps:

1. Identify the subject.
2. Establish the dividing principle: consider how you are looking at the subject to separate it into parts.
3. Divide or separate the subject into the individual parts or elements based on the dividing principle.
4. Explain each part or element as it relates to the subject.

Suppose you were analyzing a hamburger, you can analyze it one way by following this process.

1. **Subject:** a cheeseburger
2. **Dividing principle:** cheeseburger as a heart-clogging meal

3. **Parts:** greasy cheese, fatty meat patty, calorie- and sodium-laden bread buns
4. **Explanation of each part:**
   1. Greasy cheese contains too much fat from milk derivatives, which build plaque in the heart.
   2. Meat patty is made up of 90% fat, which increases the bad cholesterol and the triglycerides in the heart, slow down the heart's function, and block arteries.
   3. The bread is made of white flour; this requires the body to produce more insulin in breaking it down, which affects the blood flowing through the heart.

Here is another way to analyze the same subject:

1. **Subject:** a cheeseburger
2. **Dividing principle:** cheeseburger as a scrumptious gastronomical delight
3. **Parts:** silky cheese; juicy meat patty; soft, fresh bread; and delicious vegetables
4. **Explanation of each part:**
   1. Meat patty is well-cooked and juicy.
   2. Fresh bread is soft and spongy.
   3. Vegetables like onions, tomatoes, and lettuce add a tangy, crunchy crispness to every bite.

GENERIC PLAN FOR AN ANALYSIS BY DIVISION ESSAY

Introduction Paragraph
    Thesis = Focused Topic + Dividing Principle
Supporting Paragraph 1: Part 1
    Development Sentences (or FRIEDs)
Supporting Paragraph 2: Part 2
    Development Sentences (or FRIEDs)
Supporting Paragraph 3: Part 3
    Development Sentences (or FRIEDs)
Conclusion Paragraph

Introduction Paragraph

In an analysis by division essay, the introduction provides appropriate information about the focused topic while capturing the reader's interest. A good way to start an introduction paragraph for analysis by division is to define the term being analyzed or to provide background information about it. Refer to Chapter Two for a complete list of ways to write an introduction paragraph.

Thesis Statement

The thesis statement in an analysis by division essay clearly shows what the topic is and what dividing principle is used. You should use phrases such as *To be effective as a . . ., On the basis of . . .,* or *As a . . . .*

> As a meal, a cheeseburger includes several heart-clogging foods such as the fatty meat patty, the greasy cheese, and the carbohydrate-laden bun. Several elements make a cheeseburger a heart-clogging meal.

 MEMORY TIP

Thesis Statement = Focused Topic + Dividing Principle + Parts

OR

Focused Topic + Dividing Principle

BUILDING SKILLS 6-1: Recognizing Effective Analysis by Division Thesis Statements

Read each sentence and write *TS* next to the ones that are effective analysis by division thesis statements and *X* next to those that are not effective analysis by division thesis statements.

1. A newspaper is divided into the sports section, the news section, and the classified section. _____

2. The lyrics, the singer's voice, and the musical arrangements of the song *Beautiful* make it a work of art. _____

3. The zones of the sea. _____

4. On domestic violence calls, my police roles include therapist, facilitator, and law enforcer. _____

5. Inspiring a shared vision, enabling others to act, and modeling the way are important traits in an effective leader. _____

6. Lies can have three themes: lies by omission, white lies, and blatant lies. _____

7. The pressure college students face can be divided into three parts: financial, social, and mental. _____

8. Men are different from women. _____

9. The key components of a championship sports team are hard-working players, a supportive coach, and consistent practice. _____

10. The singer's life, the message behind the lyrics, and the musical arrangement are important parts of an influential song. _____

Supporting Paragraphs

In division, your individual parts make up the focus of each of the supporting paragraphs of your essay. Arrange the parts logically and distinctly. There is no order of importance in a division essay, so you are at liberty to place your parts in any order you want.

TRANSITIONS USED IN ANALYSIS BY DIVISION ESSAYS

one part	first part	one element	area
another part	second part	another element	category
last part	third part	final element	section

BUILDING SKILLS 6-2: Choosing Useful and Logical Parts for Support

With the given topics and dividing principle, list useful parts for each topic.

1. Topic: Person
   Dividing Principle: Effective as a student
   Part 1:   Time management skills
   Part 2:   _____
   Part 3:   _____

➡

2. Topic: Friend
   Dividing Principle: Supportive friend
       Part 1:   Listens attentively
       Part 2: _____
       Part 3: _____
       Part 4: _____

3. Topic: Doctor
   Dividing Principle: Effective as a surgeon
       Part 1:   Precision skills
       Part 2: _____
       Part 3: _____
       Part 4: _____

Development Sentences

For each part of your chosen subject, readers need specific examples, details, and facts that explain how that part contributes to the subject and the dividing principle. Your main parts will be only as good as the details you use in explaining them. Your details need to be in complete sentences that give clear, sufficient, and specific information about why and how each part relates to the thesis sentence.

Remember that development information comes from many sources such as personal experience, observations, facts, statistics, case studies, memories, and more. Although there is no set length, no prescribed number of lines or sentences for development sentences, they need to be long enough to accomplish their purpose of explaining each topic sentence and short enough to be interesting. A good strategy to follow is to use a variety of development sentences (or FRIEDs) to explain each part clearly for your reader and to use roughly an equal amount of development sentences. A development sentence for the supporting paragraph about the fatty meat could be how the fat in the meat is broken down into cholesterol and triglycerides in the blood, which attaches itself to the heart and clogs the arteries.

Conclusion Paragraph

The objective of the conclusion paragraph is to end the discussion, so in an analysis by division essay, summarize the parts used in the body paragraphs in the order in which they were presented and reword the thesis statement in your conclusion. In addition, consider offering a thoughtful observation or remark in your conclusion

The fatty meat, the greasy cheese, and the carb-laden buns are elements in a cheeseburger that make it a heart-clogging meal. Many people are fans of Jimmy Buffet's "Cheeseburger in Paradise" song and believe "cheeseburger is paradise," but the reality is, it is a heart attack in paradise.

EXAMPLE OF AN ANALYSIS BY DIVISION ESSAY

Note: This essay has in-text citations. Refer to Chapter Twelve for explanation about citations.

Heart Attack in Paradise

The cheeseburger is the quintessential American meal found at most restaurants and barbeques. But as good as it tastes, it plays havoc with your metabolism. According to cardiologist Dr. Tom Grundy, in the hours after consuming a cheeseburger, wild swings of blood sugar and blood fats occur (9). These swings cause the body to discharge hazardous chemicals that damage the walls of arteries in the heart. In fact, the typical American cheeseburger contains several dangerous ingredients that make it a heart-clogging, heart-attack-waiting-to-happen meal.

One deadly ingredient in a cheeseburger is the greasy cheese. The cheeses most commonly used with hamburgers are Cheddar, Swiss, or American. Dr. Tony Hage, a registered nutritionist, noted that cheese is made from milk, which is high in protein, calcium, saturated fat, and acid (25). For the cheese to ferment, certain chemicals are added, which adds to its fat content. In a 2009 study, the American Heart Association reported that many people think of calcium-rich cheese as healthful, but "in reality it is a dangerous trap because just one ounce of full-fat cheese can have as much as six grams of artery-clogging fat—a third of a day's daily intake of saturated fat" (3). The higher the saturated fat, the higher the risk of heart attack or stroke (Grundy 16).

Another dangerous ingredient in a cheeseburger is the fatty meat patty. In most hamburgers, beef or red meat is used. Often it is the "red meat with a 90 % fat content, which means only 10% of that meat is lean or free of white fat" (Hage 12). The American Heart Association recommends that the average person consume lean red meat "the size of a deck of cards to stay below the 20 grams of daily intake of saturated fat" (3). One greasy, fatty meat patty in a cheeseburger may very well account for most of the saturated fat needed daily. More importantly, as the red meat is broken down in the body, it is processed into cholesterol and triglycerides in the blood that attach themselves to the heart and clog the arteries, which in turn raise the blood pressure level and the likelihood of a heart attack or stroke (Grundy 11).

The last risky ingredient in a cheeseburger is the carbohydrate-laden bun. Foods high in carbohydrates include the starches like bread, pasta, rice, and potatoes. Dr. Hage confirms that simple carbohydrates or starches are digested quickly and turn into sugar—high insulin—in the bloodstream (13).

He adds that the high insulin levels turn into body fat, which increases the production of the bad cholesterol and triglycerides (15). Cholesterol and triglycerides attach more plaque, a sticky substance, to the arteries of the heart, causing heart blockage (Grundy, 21). While the body needs carbohydrates for energy, it needs a minimal amount daily, and the large bun in a cheeseburger is an excessive amount of carbohydrates for one meal.

The typical American cheeseburger contains greasy cheese, fatty meat, and carbohydrate-laden bread; all these elements make this a heart-clogging, heart-attack-waiting-to-happen meal. Many people are fans of Jimmy Buffet's "Cheeseburger in Paradise" song and believe a "cheeseburger **is** paradise," but the reality is it is "a heart attack in paradise."

Works Cited

American Heart Association. *American Heart Association*, AHA, 2011. Web. 11 Jan. 2010.

Grundy, Tom. *The Low-fat, Low-cholesterol Diet*. New York: Wiley, 2010. Print.

Hage, Tony. *Nutrition and Fast Food*. New York: Farrar, 2009. Print.

❚ BUILDING SKILLS TOGETHER 6-1: Evaluating an Analysis by Division Essay

Working in a small group, read the following essay and answer the evaluation questions that follow.

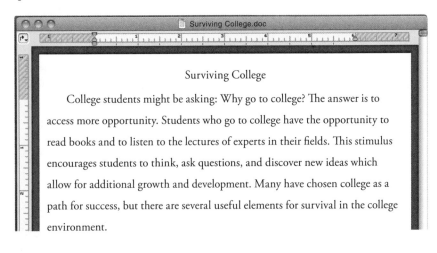

Surviving College

College students might be asking: Why go to college? The answer is to access more opportunity. Students who go to college have the opportunity to read books and to listen to the lectures of experts in their fields. This stimulus encourages students to think, ask questions, and discover new ideas which allow for additional growth and development. Many have chosen college as a path for success, but there are several useful elements for survival in the college environment.

One useful element for college survival is good study habits. Effective study habits include prereading the material before it is lectured on, taking good notes, and doing all the assignments on time. Note taking can help in preparing for a test. The notes can be made into flashcards to help with memorization. Another good habit is working with study groups where a number of students meet and go over the material and test one another. Studying in groups has always been a great way to learn complex subjects. Students learning from students helps with information retention.

College survival needs time management. Managing time wisely will help decrease stress about the little time-consuming aspects of college, such as finding parking, walking to class, meeting teachers, and reading notes. Students should allow enough time to get to school and to find parking. Also, every day, students should set aside study time to finish the day's assignments, stay prepared, and not miss valuable information.

The third element to college survival is class involvement. Class involvement tests students' comprehension of the learned material. It also allows for more engagement with other students and the teacher; therefore, students become more excited about coming to class. Work in groups allows students to compare notes with others. Classroom involvement will increase students' confidence in public speaking as well as improve material retention.

Study habits, time management, and class involvement are three useful elements for college survival. The college path to success is not easy, but it is possible if students know how to survive in that environment. As Henry Ford once said, "Obstacles are those frightful things you see when you take your eyes off your goal."

1. Consider the introduction. What method is used to "hook" the reader's interest? Does the introduction offer sufficient introductory sentences about the topic?

2. Underline the thesis statement. What is the focused topic or opinion? Does it indicate an analysis by division pattern? Is the thesis statement effective? What might you change or add?

_____

_____

_____

3. How many supporting paragraphs are used to develop the thesis? What order are they in?

_____

_____

_____

_____

4. Do the supporting paragraphs provide strong support or explanation of the thesis statement? Why or why not?

_____

_____

_____

5. Consider the development sentences (or FRIEDs) in each supporting paragraph. How many and which ones are used in each paragraph? Are they effective? Explain your answer.

_____

_____

_____

6. Circle the transition words or expressions. What order (time, space, or importance) is used to guide the reader from element or part to element or part? How effective are the transitions?

_____

_____

_____

7. Is there a conclusion paragraph? How does it end the essay's discussion? What method(s) (restating, observing, remarking, or summarizing) is used to conclude? Explain your answer.

_____

_____

_____

8. What point of view is used in the essay? Is it relevant to the writer's purpose? Is it consistent throughout the essay?

_____

_____

_____

9. Is the title effective? Why or why not?

_____

_____

_____

SUGGESTED TOPICS FOR WRITING ANALYSIS BY DIVISION ESSAYS

Choose one of the following topics or use one of your own and then use prewriting techniques to develop your draft for an analysis by division essay.

A popular song	A book or story you have read
A sports team	An athlete
A company or warehouse	An admired boss or manager
Effective customer service	A teacher
A successful group project for a class	A machine such as a computer or camera

BUILDING SKILLS TOGETHER 6-2: Analysis by Division Essay Feedback Checklist

Once the rough draft of your analysis by division essay is completed, have a partner read it and answer the following revision and editing questions. You may also use this checklist to revise and edit your own essay.

Revising Essay Structure

☐ Does the introduction capture the attention of the reader? Are there sufficient introductory sentences about the subject? What changes might you make?

☐ Underline the thesis. Does it include an opinion on the topic and an indication of analysis by division? What changes might you make?

☐ Are clear, specific, and related elements or parts used as supporting paragraphs? What changes might you make?

☐ Is each supporting element or part sufficiently developed with enough development sentences (or FRIEDs)? Where can you make improvements?

☐ Are clear transition words used to move you through the body paragraphs from element or part to element or part? Where might you make changes?

☐ Does the conclusion end the essay's discussion? What concluding method (restating, observing, remarking, or summarizing) is used? What changes might you make?

☐ Is the point of view in the essay consistent and relevant? Are any changes needed?

☐ How effective is the title in capturing the essay's content? Why or why not?

Editing Spelling, Diction, and Sentence Construction

☐ Are there any misspelled words?

☐ Are appropriate and specific words used?

☐ Are any slang words, text message language, or clichés used?

☐ Consider sentence structure and correct any errors with:

    ☐ Fragments, run-ons, and comma splices

    ☐ Misplaced or dangling modifiers

    ☐ Verb tense consistency

    ☐ Pronoun agreement

    ☐ Subject and verb agreement

Refer to Appendix A for a review of grammar concepts.

Final Assessment

☐ What do you like the most about the essay?

☐ What are you unclear about or have difficulty with in the essay?

CHAPTER SEVEN: Comparison or Contrast
Building Essays with Similarities or Differences

Is a frozen dinner as healthy as a home-cooked dinner? If not, what makes them different? Does a new coffeemaker offer similar benefits to the one you have? Many of us comparison shop before we buy or do something to determine similarities and differences or pros and cons before we spend money. In many college courses, like psychology, history, business, or chemistry, you may be asked to write a comparison or contrast analysis on discipline-specific subjects.

When you write a comparison or contrast essay, you show how two people, two places, two things, or two ideas are similar or different. You place the topics next to each other to evaluate the similarities or differences. **Comparison** means to compare and presents the similarities between two topics, whereas **contrast** shows the differences. Generally, the word *compare* is used to mean compare or contrast, but in this book, *compare* means only to look at similarities. However, check with your instructor as each discipline has its own requirements.

WRITING A COMPARISON OR CONTRAST ESSAY

To write a comparison or contrast essay, choose two topics that are comparable or have something in common, so you can develop points of comparison or contrast. An example of two comparable topics could be the iPod Shuffle and the iPod Nano since both are portable media players but with different features. Once you have selected your topics, follow these steps:

1. Decide on the focus or purpose you want to emphasize; similarities or differences.
2. List points of similarities or differences between the two topics.

3. Select several similarities or differences to use as supporting points/
   paragraphs
4. Organize the supporting points in order.

There are two different orders you can choose when writing a comparison or contrast essay: the **point-by-point** (PBP) order or the **topic-by-topic** (TBT) order.

The **point-by-point** presents one point of similarity or difference at a time about both topics and then moves to the next point. It is better suited for college writing and will be the focus of this chapter.

GENERIC PLAN FOR POINT-BY-POINT ORDER

Introduction Paragraph
Thesis = Focused Topic (Topic A + Topic B are similar or different)
  Support Paragraph 1: Point 1: Similarity or Difference 1
    Topic A: Development Sentences (or FRIEDs)
    Topic B: Development Sentences (or FRIEDs)
  Support Paragraph 2: Point 2: Similarity or Difference 2
    Topic A: Development Sentences (or FRIEDs)
    Topic B: Development Sentences (or FRIEDs)
  Support Paragraph 3: Point 3: Similarity or Difference 3
    Topic A: Development Sentences (or FRIEDs)
    Topic B: Development Sentences (or FRIEDs)
Conclusion Paragraph

The **topic-by-topic** order presents all the points about the first topic and then all the points about the second topic. This pattern yields a two-paragraph essay and may be too simplistic for college writing.

GENERIC PLAN FOR TOPIC-BY-TOPIC ORDER

Introduction Paragraph
Thesis = Focused Topic (Topic A + Topic B are similar or different)
  Support Paragraph 1: Topic A
    Point 1 & Development Sentences (or FRIEDs)
    Point 2 & Development Sentences (or FRIEDs)
    Point 3 & Development Sentences (or FRIEDs)
  Support Paragraph 2: Topic B
    Point 1 & Development Sentences (or FRIEDs)
    Point 2 & Development Sentences (or FRIEDs)
    Point 3 & Development Sentences (or FRIEDs)
Conclusion Paragraph

Consider the following topics for a comparison or contrast essay.

iPod Shuffle and the iPod Nano

Similarities	Differences
compact media devices	video capabilities
play music	size
compatible with iTunes software	physical features
memory capacity	blue tooth connectivity
download capabilities	

Now, choose to analyze either similarities or differences. It is usually easier to show how things are different from each other, so for this example, consider the differences between the media players as a focus.

BUILDING SKILLS 7-1: Finding Points of Similarities or Contrasts

List two similarities and two differences under the topics; then, choose which side you would focus on to analyze the topics.

1. Topics: basketball and football

    Similarities   Differences

    _____   _____

    _____   _____

    _____   _____

    　　　　Focus: _____

2. Topics: American and Mexican finger foods

    Similarities   Differences

    _____   _____

    _____   _____

    _____   _____

    　　　　Focus: _____

3. Topics: electric and gas cars

Similarities	Differences
_____	_____
_____	_____
_____	_____

Focus: _____

4. Topics: men's and women's attitudes about dating

Similarities	Differences
_____	_____
_____	_____
_____	_____

Focus: _____

Introduction Paragraph

In a comparison or contrast essay, the introduction provides appropriate information about the focused topics while engaging the reader's interest. A good way to start an introduction paragraph for comparison is to provide enough background information about topic A and topic B.

Thesis Statement

The thesis statement in a comparison or contrast essay includes the two topics and a statement about purpose or whether the writer is comparing or contrasting them. Be careful not to state that one topic is better because that is the argumentation pattern of writing instead of the comparison or contrast pattern.

 MEMORY TIP

Thesis = Focused Topic (Topic A and Topic B + are similar)

Apple's iPod Shuffle and the iPod Nano share several clear similarities.

Thesis = Focused Topic (Topic A and Topic B + are different)

Although both the Shuffle and the Nano are iPods, they differ from each other as portable media players.

BUILDING SKILLS 7-2: Recognizing Effective Comparison or Contrast Thesis Statements

Read each sentence and write *TS* next to the ones that are effective comparison or contrast thesis statements and *X* next to those that are not effective comparison or contrast thesis statements.

1. There are several differences between college and university. _____

2. Waterskiing is better than snow skiing. _____

3. Men and women communicate differently. _____

4. Diets are not that useful. _____

5. There are several similarities between my sister and aunt. _____

6. Smokers are more likely to die from lung cancer than nonsmokers. _____

7. Vegetarians and meat eaters are different in their values, their food preferences, and their health concerns. _____

8. The engineering in Japanese cars is different from that in German cars. _____

9. Paradise Burgers is a better restaurant than Corner Burgery. _____

10. Playing basketball is different from being a spectator at a basketball game. _____

BUILDING SKILLS 7-3: Writing Comparison or Contrast Thesis Statements

Prewrite for each topic, and on the lines below write a strong thesis statement with a clear comparison or contrast focus for each topic.

1. Two college classroom environments

_____

_____

2. Two leaders

_____

_____

3. Two supermarkets

_____

_____

4. Dating and fishing

_____

_____

5. Fighting on a battlefield and driving in traffic

_____

_____

Supporting Paragraphs

The supporting paragraphs in a comparison or contrast essay are selected from the points of similarities or points of differences that you listed in brainstorming the two topics. You can present and develop the supporting paragraphs either by using point-by-point order or topic-by-topic order although the preferred method for college writing is point-by-point order. There is no order of importance in a comparison or contrast essay so long as the points are organized in a logical manner. The differences between the Shuffle and the Nano are the supporting paragraphs. You can discuss all four points or eliminate one to make your discussion shorter. Your supporting paragraphs might include the following topic sentences:

Supporting paragraph 1: **The first difference between the iPod's Shuffle and Nano is the physical features.**

Supporting paragraph 2: **Another difference between the iPod's Shuffle and Nano is the video capabilities.**

Supporting paragraph 3: **The third difference between the iPod's Shuffle and Nano is the blue tooth connectivity.**

TRANSITIONS USED IN COMPARISON AND CONTRAST ESSAYS

one similarity	another similarity	a third similarity	
one difference	another difference	a third difference	
similarly	likewise, like	however	both
in contrast	unlike	while	on the other hand
in comparison	nevertheless	whereas	on the contrary

Consult Appendix B for a complete list of transitions.

Development Sentences

Each point of similarity (or difference) needs to have development sentences that show how Topic A then Topic B relates to each point of similarity (or difference). You decide the order of the topics, but whatever you choose to have as Topic A for the first point of similarity (or difference), you must use it as Topic A for all subsequent points of similarity (or difference). This consistency is crucial so readers do not get confused about which topic you are discussing. Be sure to use a variety of development sentences (or FRIEDs) for each of the topics. Using the example of the Shuffle and the Nano, your development may look like this:

Supporting paragraph 1: **The first difference is the physical features.**

Topic A: The Shuffle's features	Development sentences (or FRIEDs)
Topic B: The Nano's features	Development sentences (or FRIEDs)

Supporting paragraph 2: **The second difference is the video capabilities.**

Topic A: The Shuffle's video	Development sentences (or FRIEDs)
Topic B: The Nano's video capabilities	Development sentences (or FRIEDs)

Supporting paragraph 3: **The third difference is the bluetooth connectivity.**

Topic A: The Shuffle's bluetooth capabilities	Development sentences (or FRIEDs)
Topic B: The Nano's bluetooth capabilities	Development sentences (or FRIEDs)

✖ BUILDING TIP

If you do not use enough development sentences (or FRIEDs) in the point-by-point order, the readers may experience a "ping-pong" effect that makes your writing boring. To avoid that, develop each supporting sentence thoroughly with enough development sentences.

Conclusion Paragraph

The objective of the conclusion is to end the discussion, so restate, in the order they were presented, the points of similarities or differences and reword the thesis statement. You may offer a thoughtful observation or remark in your conclusion so long as you restate the thesis statement. Remember not to start a new idea.

Physical features, video capabilities, and blue tooth connectivity are several differences between the *iPod Shuffle* and the *iPod Nano*. Regardless

of which is chosen, both portable devices allow the listener to, in the words of iPod addicts, "Shake, shuffle, and roll the groove thing" any time (Biersdorfer 3).

EXAMPLE OF A COMPARISON OR CONTRAST ESSAY

Note: This essay has in-text citations. Refer to Chapter Twelve for a complete guide on quotations and citations.

Anytime Music

In October 2001, Apple launched its innovatively designed and aggressively marketed brand of portable media players called iPod. Since then there has been a considerable change in the makeup of the digital and music industries. Technology expert Paul Smythe confirms that based on the worldwide sales numbers, the iPod is the best-selling digital audio player in history (qtd. in Biersdorfer). The iPod is a portable media player used for downloading music, videos, and Web-based applications such as e-mail. The iPod product line features four different products including the Shuffle and the Nano. Although the Shuffle and the Nano share many similarities as iPods, they have several significant differences.

The first difference between the iPod Shuffle and Nano is the physical features. The Shuffle is compact, measuring 1 inch high by 1.62 inches wide and weighs less than 1 ounce ("Reviews–iPod Shuffle"). It has a built-in clip in the back for the user to attach it to key chains, handbags, gym shorts, belts, or shirtsleeves. It has no screen in the front, just a white circle with four arrows to denote the functions of *play, pause, forward, or rewind*. It comes in five colors: blue, red, green, grey, and pink. On the other hand, the iPod Nano is small but not as compact as the Shuffle. It measures 3.6 inches high by 1.5 inches wide and weighs 1.3 ounces ("Reviews and Rankings"). It has a 2-inch screen display in the front with a white circle of functions like the Shuffle. It can be carried in the palm of a hand and is as pencil-slim as a business card case holder. It comes in nine colors: purple, red, green, blue, white, pink, black, silver, and yellow.

The second difference between the iPod Shuffle and Nano is the video capabilities. The Shuffle can hold 500 songs, but has no screen display or video function. On the other hand, the Nano holds up from 2,000 to 4,000 songs, up to 14,000 viewable photos, and up to 16 hours of video ("Reviews and Rankings"). It has a crisp and vivid 2-inch widescreen LCD display with a high-resolution picture for watching movies, TV shows, and videos. The LCD screen makes it easier to view song selections and to watch music videos while listening to the selected songs. Furthermore, you can view picture-perfect photos and watch music videos.

The third difference between the iPod Shuffle and Nano is the blue tooth connectivity. Blue tooth is a wireless radio technology that allows electronic devices to connect to one another. Blue tooth makes short-range connections just like cables connect a computer to a keyboard, mouse, or printer. The Shuffle is designed to be the easiest and fastest way to build an ultra-organized music collection jukebox, but it can only be connected to a computer via a USB dock and has no built-in blue tooth technology for use elsewhere (Hart-Davis 120). In contrast, the Nano has strong blue tooth capabilities as it could be charged via a USB dock or a blue tooth transmitter (Hart-Davis 200). For car use, the Nano can be connected through a wireless transmitter with a built-in rechargeable battery, a receiver chord, a power adapter, and an audio cable. In that way, the Nano helps make music and video collections highly versatile, easily accessible, and efficiently portable.

The iPod Shuffle and Nano are different in physical features, video capabilities, and blue tooth connectivity. Regardless of which is chosen, both portable devices allow the listener to, in the words of iPod addicts, "Shake, shuffle, and roll the groove thing" any time (Biersdorfer 3).

Works Cited

Biersdorfer, J. D. *iPod Shuffle Fan Book: Life Is a Playlist*. Sebastopol: O'Reilly Media, 2005. Print.

Hart-Davis, Guy. *How to Do Everything: iPod & Itunes*. New York: McGraw-Hill, 2008. Print.

"Reviews and Rankings - Apple iPod Nano." *Pc World*. 25 Nov. 2007: 74. Print.

"Reviews - iPod Shuffle." *Macworld: The Macintosh Magazine*. 29 Nov. 2007: 36. Print.

◆ BUILDING SKILLS TOGETHER 7-1: Evaluating a Comparison or Contrast Essay

Working in a small group, read the following essay and answer the evaluation questions that follow. Note that this essay has in-text citations. Please refer to Chapter Twelve for a complete guide on quotations and citations.

➡

Humble Fame.doc

Humble Fame

Baseball is a bat-and-ball sport where two teams of nine players go against each other. Over the decades there have been many great baseball players such as the "Babe" or Babe Ruth, who was an American Major League baseball player from 1914–1935 (Montville 43). In the twenties, his prowess at hitting home runs and magnetic personality made him an American icon. In recent years, more great players have come about like Mark McGwire of the St. Louis Cardinals. Babe Ruth of the Yankees and Mark McGwire of the Cardinals share several similarities.

The first similarity between the two great baseball players is their humble beginnings. Babe Ruth was not always a slugger, but he gained great strength from playing street ball with his friends. Interestingly, Babe was always getting into trouble. In fact, he landed in a detention center where he learned how to bat correctly. At the detention center he was coached in baseball, and Babe fell in love with the sport (Montville 65). As Babe grew older, he worked hard to get plate appearances. Likewise, Mark McGwire started playing baseball as young child. He attended Damien High School in La Verne, California, where he won honors for playing baseball (Rains 89). He went on to play college baseball; then he made it into the majors where he started with the Angels.

The second similarity between Babe Ruth and Mark McGwire is money. Babe did not always have money. He started making money when he made it to the majors. After Babe made a name in the majors, he was traded to a few different teams, and that was when he started making a lot of money. When he finally started to "crush the ball," hitting homeruns, he began making more money (Angell). Likewise, Mark made it to the majors, but he was not financially secure and had to work hard to get playing time. More playing time meant more money made. Mark was traded to the Cardinals, and that is where he made his mark ("Jocks"). This is where he became more popular with his hitting ability, so his salary went up.

Fame was part of their lives. Babe Ruth held the record for 34 years for the most home runs (Montville 95). He was known for his hitting abilities and was inducted into the Hall of Fame for his outstanding achievements in baseball. He was linked with numerous Hollywood stars and was well loved by the public. Mark McGwire has also set records for hitting and was placed in the Hall of Fame for his single season of seventy-two homeruns (Rains 110). Also, Mark was a great asset to the Cardinals as a first-baseman.

Humble beginnings, money, and fame are three similarities between Babe Ruth and Mark McGwire. Baseball will always remain an exhilarating sport, and while baseball players come and go, the great ones will never be forgotten. To be great, in the words of Babe Ruth, "Don't let the fear of striking out hold you back" (Angell).

Works Cited

Angell, Roger. "Shouts & Murmurs – Babe Ruth: My Teammate, My Lover." *The New Yorker*, 12 Feb. 2002: 45. Print.

Montville, Leigh. *The Big Bam: The Life and Times of Babe Ruth*. New York: Doubleday, 2006. Print.

Rains, Rob. *Mark McGwire, Home Run Hero*. New York: St. Martin's Press, 1998. Print.

"Jocks - Mark McGwire Bashes His Way into Baseball History." *People Weekly*, 12 Jan. 1998: 180. Print.

1. Consider the introduction. What method is used to "hook" the reader's interest? Does the introduction offer sufficient introductory sentences about the topic?

   _____

   _____

   _____

2. Underline the thesis statement. What is the focused topic or opinion? Is the thesis statement effective? What might you change or add?

   _____

   _____

   _____

3. How many supporting paragraphs are used to develop the thesis? What order are they in?

4. Do the supporting paragraphs provide strong support or explanation of the thesis statement? Why or why not?

5. Consider the development sentences (or FRIEDs) in each supporting paragraph. How many and which ones are used in each paragraph? Are they effective? Explain your answer.

6. Circle the transition words or expressions. What order (time, space, or importance) is used to guide the reader from one similarity (or difference) to another? How effective are the transitions?

7. Is there a conclusion paragraph? How does it end the essay's discussion? What method(s) (restating, observing, remarking, or summarizing) is used to conclude? Explain your answer.

8. What point of view is used in the essay? Is it relevant to the writer's purpose? Is it consistent throughout the essay?

9. Is the title effective? Why or why not?

_____

_____

_____

SUGGESTED TOPICS FOR WRITING COMPARISON OR CONTRAST ESSAYS

Choose one of the following topics or use one of your own and then use pre-writing techniques to develop your draft for a comparison or contrast essay.

The role of women in any two ethnic cultures	Any two artists
Any two approaches to studying	Any two successful business executives
Two different businesses selling the same product	Two neighborhoods
Two bosses	Two youth groups
Two parenting approaches	A novel and a movie that tell the same story

● BUILDING SKILLS TOGETHER 7-2: Comparison or Contrast Essay Feedback Checklistt

Once the rough draft of your comparison or contrast essay is completed, have a partner read it and answer the following revision and editing questions. You may also use this checklist to revise and edit your own essay.

Revising Essay Structure

☐ Does the introduction capture the attention of the reader? Are there sufficient introductory sentences before the thesis statement? What changes might you make?

☐ Underline the thesis. Does it include an opinion on the topic and an indication of comparison or contrast? What changes might you make?

☐ Are clear, specific, and related similarities or differences used as supporting paragraphs? What could you improve on?

☐ Is each supporting similarity or difference sufficiently developed with enough development sentences (or FRIEDs)? What might you change?

☐ Are clear transition words used to move you through the body paragraphs from one similarity or difference to another? Where might you make changes?

☐ Does the conclusion end the essay's discussion? What concluding method (restating, observing, remarking, or summarizing) is used? What changes might you make?

☐ Is the point of view in the essay consistent and relevant? Are any changes needed?

☐ How effective is the title in capturing the essay's content? Why or why not?

Editing Spelling, Diction, and Sentence Construction

☐ Are there any misspelled words?

☐ Are appropriate and specific words used?

☐ Are any slang words, text message language, or clichés used?

☐ Consider sentence structure and correct any errors with:

  ☐ Fragments, run-ons, and comma splices

  ☐ Misplaced or dangling modifiers

  ☐ Verb tense consistency

  ☐ Pronoun agreement

  ☐ Subject and verb agreement

Refer to Appendix A for a review of grammar concepts.

Final Assessment

☐ What do you like the most about the essay?

☐ What are you unclear about or have difficulty with in the essay?

UNIT THREE: Building Loosely Structured Essays

T HE ESSAYS PRESENTED in the following chapters do not follow a prescribed or formal structure when it comes to stating thesis statements, organizing supporting paragraphs, using development sentences, or presenting conclusion paragraphs. For each of the following patterns, you will use different ways of stating your thesis statement, structuring supporting paragraphs and development sentences, and concluding your essays. The patterns of writing that lend themselves to informal structures are:

- Description: Writing with Imagery
- Narration: Writing to Tell a Story
- Definition: Writing to Clarify
- Literary Analysis: Writing about Literature

CHAPTER EIGHT: Description
Building Essays with Imagery

Sometimes you understand something better when someone describes it to you. For example, your friend may describe the decorations at the party she attended last night or your history teacher may describe an important battle from the past. In many college classes, you are required to write descriptions of certain subjects.

Description creates a picture with words to help the reader see a person, place, object, or event. It selects details that build a sensory experience that *shows* rather than tells the topic. The purpose is to make the readers feel as if they are in that room with you or facing that person or holding that object. With the use of detailed word imagery, you are able to bring a person, place, or object to life for the reader.

WRITING A DESCRIPTION ESSAY

The main thrust of description is the impression you are trying to convey to the reader. The main impression or **dominant impression** is the overall sense, image, or effect you want to create for the readers through your sensory details or five senses. To write a description essay:

1. Focus on a topic: a place, person, object, or event.
2. Engage the five senses—sight, sound, taste, smell, and touch—and prewrite ideas or images that come to mind about your topic. Use **objective** (factual) and **subjective** (personal reactions) description.
3. Look at the ideas in your prewriting and join those that seem to go together; then, see what overall mood they convey to you. That mood would be your dominant impression.
4. Decide what sensory details you will keep and what order of organization you will use to start your description. You might use **spatial** or **space order** in describing a person, place, or object, but you might use **time order** in describing an event.

5. Start writing a draft, being careful to use order and as much detailed sensory images as you can to support your dominant impression. Consider this list for generic sensory details.

Sight	colors shapes sizes patterns brightness
Sound	loud/soft piercing/soothing
Smell	sweet/sour sharp/mild cloying pungent
Taste	bitter sugary metallic spicy
Touch	hard/soft delicate/rough dry/oily smooth silky

6. Consider using similes and metaphors. Similes and metaphors both call attention to how two different things are similar. These powerful descriptive tools help you make a familiar thing look, sound, feel, or behave like something else. They enable you to draw parallels between topics to clarify concepts for the reader and to conjure up images that are more instantly descriptive than a long section of writing.

A **simile** helps readers picture one thing as like another thing. A simile uses explicit comparison words such as *like* or *as*.

Simile: Life is like a highway.

On the other hand, a **metaphor** does not use direct comparison words. The metaphor goes a step further than the simile and instead of asking readers to picture one thing as being like another, readers picture one thing as *being* another.

Metaphor: Life is a highway.

MEMORY TIP

There are no rules about when you should a simile versus a metaphor. It depends on the effect you are trying to achieve. You can remember the difference between similes and metaphors by remembering that a *simile* has the letter *I* in it, just like the word *like*, which you often use in a simile.

GENERIC PLAN FOR A DESCRIPTION ESSAY

Although there is no set structure for descriptive writing, here is a generic plan of what a description essay might look like.

Introduction Paragraph
  Thesis = Focused Topic (Topic + Dominant Impression)
Support Paragraph 1: First sensory image
  Development Sentences using any or all of the five senses
Support Paragraph 2: Another sensory image
  Development Sentences using any or all of the five senses
Support Paragraph 3: Another sensory image
  Development Sentences using any or all of the five senses
Conclusion Paragraph
  Restate the dominant impression
  Final observation

Consider the topic of my bedroom for a description essay. Prewrite by listing sensory details or details for sight, smell, sound, taste, and touch.

sight: queen-sized mahogany bed, soft, aquamarine-blue walls, colorful and flowery bedspread, flower arrangement, tall, mahogany dresser, cluttered working desk with a tall lamp, black iPod sound station, strewn shoes, posters of idols, television, computer, books, dog's bed in corner

touch: the soft, fuzzy bedspread, crisp linens

smell: vanilla-scented air from the candle, musty smell of worn shoes, socks, and sleep

sound: brush of the palm tree limbs against the window pane, soothing classical music from iPod, serenity, soft-spinning hum of the ceiling fan blades

taste: nothing applies

Introduction Paragraph

A good way to start an introduction paragraph for description is to provide interesting and relevant information about the topic of the essay. If the topic is about a person, you may briefly explain the relationship you have with that person. For example, maybe you choose to describe your father because he is a courageous and admirable man. If the topic is a place, you may explain when you saw it and why it is important to you. If the topic is an object, explain its value to you.

Thesis Statement

Your thesis statement in a description essay contains the topic (person, place, object, or event) and the dominant impression. Generally, the dominant impression is one or two words that show the overall sense you want to leave the reader with about your topic.

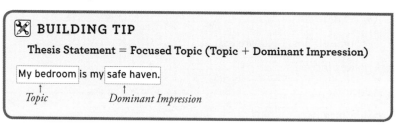

BUILDING TIP

Thesis Statement = Focused Topic (Topic + Dominant Impression)

My bedroom is my safe haven.

    ↑   ↑

  Topic   *Dominant Impression*

COMMON WORDS FOR DOMINANT IMPRESSIONS

Dominant impressions for places

crowded	inviting	drab	inspiring
tasteless	cheerful	gaudy	cozy
depressing	eerie	stuffy	dark
dazzling	restful	haunting	refuge

Dominant impressions for people

creative	angry	proud	generous
tense	silent	dependable	responsible
snobbish	shy	aggressive	witty

Dominant impressions for objects

sleek	rough	refreshing	lethal
weighty	spongy	velvety	delicate

Vague words to avoid		
good	bad	fun
nice	fine	beautiful
okay	normal	typical

BUILDING SKILLS 8-1: Dominant Impressions

State a dominant impression—one or two words—to describe each of the following phrases. You may refer to the dominant impressions listed on page 121–122.

1. The room you are now in: _____

2. A warehouse: _____

3. The home of your grandparents: _____

4. A police officer: _____

5. A doctor: _____

6. A gang member: _____

7. A cup of coffee: _____

8. An old man sitting on a porch: _____

9. A fireplace: _____

10. A baked cake: _____

Supporting Paragraphs

In description, the supporting paragraphs consist of the specific sensory images you want to create and show to convey your topic's dominant impression. The development sentences are the details involving touch, smell, taste, hearing, and sight. The more sensory details you use, the better your description. Be sure to use interesting descriptive vocabulary and stay away from overused words such as *good, bad, nice,* or *mean.* Most importantly, be sure to order your supporting paragraphs in a spatial (top to bottom, right to left, or outside to inside) or timely (first to last) sequence, so the reader can move through your description with ease. Rely heavily on transitions. If you are describing a house, you may want to describe the outside of the house and then the inside, but do not shift the details back and forth as that confuses the reader. If you are describing a person, you might want to describe the face and head and then the body. A meal can be described from the first course to the last one. In the example of the bedroom, the supporting paragraphs and development sentences would be all the sensory details listed in the brainstorm, except that you need to organize them to show the bedroom in a logical manner.

 BUILDING TIP

Since you are usually writing about your own perspective and experience in a description essay, most description essays require the use of **first-person point of view,** using the pronouns *I* or *we.*

TRANSITIONS USED IN DESCRIPTION PARAGRAPHS

Transitions are essential to a description essay because they show the organization of your details. Be sure to use them so that you move the reader logically through your details.

Order of space

from the top	to the left/right	to the back	in the corner	under	behind	next to	over
at the bottom	in the center	at the front	underneath	above	beside	outside	inside

Order of time

in the beginning	after	before	next	soon	while	then	last	finally

Consult Appendix B for a complete list of transitions.

BUILDING SKILLS 8-2: Finding Details for Support

Write three sensory details to support the dominant impression of each topic.

1. A jacket you like

_____

_____

_____

_____

2. A poorly rated, dirty restaurant

_____

_____

_____

_____

3. A busy movie theater

_____

_____

_____

_____

4. A scene from a concert or athletic event

_____

_____

_____

_____

BUILDING SKILLS 8-3: Identifying Sensory Details

Read this paragraph and identify the details that go with each of the senses; then write the dominant impression.

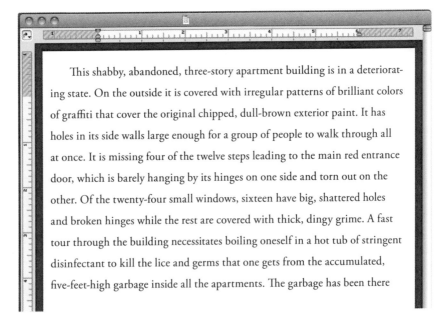

This shabby, abandoned, three-story apartment building is in a deteriorating state. On the outside it is covered with irregular patterns of brilliant colors of graffiti that cover the original chipped, dull-brown exterior paint. It has holes in its side walls large enough for a group of people to walk through all at once. It is missing four of the twelve steps leading to the main red entrance door, which is barely hanging by its hinges on one side and torn out on the other. Of the twenty-four small windows, sixteen have big, shattered holes and broken hinges while the rest are covered with thick, dingy grime. A fast tour through the building necessitates boiling oneself in a hot tub of stringent disinfectant to kill the lice and germs that one gets from the accumulated, five-feet-high garbage inside all the apartments. The garbage has been there so long that plant life has started to accumulate on it. Inside the first story are massive water puddles from the rain that comes in from the broken ceilings of the floors above and the roof. These rain puddles have become a swampy home to germ-infested critters. The acrid, noxious smells emanating inside make the eyes tear up excessively and the bile rise up in the mouth. The slightest wind that whistles through the building lifts with it the pungent smells of decay and rot; meanwhile, the scurrying of rats and mice is so loud one thinks a stampede is in progress. Throughout the interior of the building, the uneven, rotted, wood floor boards are dangerous to walk on as their complete surrender to decay is imminent. What is left of the broken, jagged, wooden stair railing is slathered with slimy green mildew.

Sight: _____

_____

Sound: _____

_____

Touch: _____

_____

Taste: _____

_____

Smell: _____

_____

Dominant Impression: _____

_____

Conclusion Paragraph

The objective of the conclusion is to end the discussion, so to end your description essay, remind the reader of the dominant impression and then make a final observation about the topic. Consider this concluding paragraph for the essay on *my bedroom*.

> The sounds and sights in my room are those of serenity and peace, and the mood in my room is one of freedom and security. While my bedroom may be untidy, it is my daily safe haven in this world.

EXAMPLE OF A DESCRIPTION ESSAY

My Sanctuary

I live with my family in a big, five-bedroom house on a quiet street. Most of my teen years have been spent in this warm and inviting home. Although I am fond of and care for the whole house, my bedroom is the one spot in the house that matters most to me. Over the years I have gone through different decors for my bedroom, but one thing has never changed: at the end of every day, my bedroom is my safe haven.

My bedroom walls are a soft, aquamarine-blue color that relaxes me. I chose to have this color on the walls because it is my favorite color; it is warm and inviting, and it matches the flowery background color on my bedspread. In the middle of the room is the queen-sized mahogany bed with the colorful blue tropical-flowered bedspread. Underneath the floral bedspread are crisp, vanilla-scented, soft blue linens. My bedspread is soft and fuzzy to the touch, but it hugs my safest place in the world, my bed.

To the left of the bed is my tall, sturdy mahogany dresser that houses six drawers filled with my clothes. Several of the clothing items in there are souvenirs from younger phases of my life. Next to that is my cluttered working desk. On my desk sit disorganized stacks of books and papers, a tall antique lamp, my laptop, and my black iPod sound station. Directly across from my bed and mounted on the wall is the 24-inch flat-screen television surrounded by seven colorful posters of my favorite bands and heroes.

To the right of my bed and over by the bedroom door sits my dog's fluffy fleece bed. Strewn all over the bedroom's cherry-colored hardwood floors are worn shoes and socks, piles of dirty laundry, and scattered textbooks. Thankfully, the vanilla-scented candle cleverly masks the dirty laundry smell. The brush of the palm tree limbs against the windowpane creates a soothing sound that accompanies the low, soft music coming from my iPod, and if I listen carefully I hear the soft-spinning hum of the ceiling fan blades.

The sounds and sights in my room are those of serenity and peace, and the mood in my room is one of freedom and security. While my room may be untidy, it is my daily safe haven in this world.

▲ BUILDING SKILLS TOGETHER 8-1: Evaluating
▌ Description Essays

Read the following essays and answer the evaluation questions that follow.

Essay One

Sugar and Spice Kitchen.doc

Sugar and Spice Kitchen

Chilled to the bone, I dashed through the cold rain to the wide front porch. I reached the oak front door, scraped the metal latch back, and stepped in. A rush of warm air wrapped around me, and the familiar smells of Granny's home—tart lemon polish and beeswax—greeted me. As I walked past the sitting room, the smells of cinnamon, brown sugar, and roasted nuts teased my nostrils. Was Granny making Easter cookies? Was it that time of year already? I paused and listened to the soft laughter coming from the kitchen. Curious, I hurried down the narrow hallway as fast as my muddy shoes allowed to the spice-filled, flour-covered kitchen.

I paused at the doorway and watched my Granny and Mom knead dough. They both wore faded yellow aprons stained with grease and flour. Sprinkles of flour covered most of the yellow-tiled counters and even the polished hardwood floor. Bowls of chopped pistachios and pecans sat in the middle of the rectangular oak kitchen table, and cans of nutmeg, cinnamon, and brown sugar stood patiently next to the bowls of nuts. Bunny-shaped cookie cutters and wooden rolling pins were scattered around the table, and a brown crock of homemade butter sat next to the glass bowl of dough. Plastic measuring cups and spoons were strewn everywhere on the counters by the sink, and two cookie sheets filled with ready-to-be-baked cookies sat by the oven.

As I walked into the kitchen, I greeted my Mom and Granny and joined Mom on the blue-cushioned oak kitchen chairs. I helped her roll more dough while the pungent smell of melting butter, brown sugar, cinnamon, and rose water filled my nostrils and tantalized my taste buds. The white ribbons of steam floating from the fresh-out-of-the -oven cookies sitting to my left caressed my lips and awakened my hunger. Under my hands the scratched, cold surface of the oak table was gritty with flour, and on my fingers the dough was warm and greasy. It rolled easily under the pin and when I sank the metal cookie cutters into it, happy bunnies emerged and smiled at me. I used the sticky chopped nutty filling to bind two cookies together into one chubby, stuffed, smiling bunny.

As we worked, we exchanged funny stories and memories, and a great warmth enveloped Granny's kitchen. All the time, the rain outside drummed steadily on the roof, and the howling wind swayed the tall pine trees by the window. We were soothed by the hiss and pop of the crackling pine logs in the hearth and the occasional squeaking from the brick oven's black iron door as Granny removed batches of cookies. I could hear the butter hiss faintly as it settled in the fresh-from-the-oven cookies.

As dusk descended and the baking was done, we gathered by the fire in the dimly lit den, sipped cinnamon-laced tea, and ate melt-in-your-mouth-like-cotton-candy Easter cookies. They smelled and tasted of sugar and spice, just like Granny's kitchen.

1. Consider the introduction. What method is used to "hook" the reader's interest? Does the introduction offer sufficient introductory sentences about the topic? What dominant impression is emphasized?

_____

_____

_____

2. What kind of sensory details are used to convey the dominant impression? Are they sufficient? How are they organized into the supporting paragraphs? What could be improved?

_____

_____

_____

3. Circle the transitional words or expressions. What order (space or time) is used to move the reader from sensory detail to another? What changes might you make?

_____

_____

_____

4. Does the conclusion restate the dominant impression and end with a final observation? How effective is it?

_____

_____

_____

5. What point of view is used in the essay? Is it relevant to the writer's purpose? Is it consistent throughout the essay?

_____

_____

_____

6. Is the title effective? Why or why not?

_____

_____

_____

Essay Two

A Photograph of Loss.doc

A Photograph of Loss

Every time I visit my sister's house, I see photographs of my mother, and I am filled with resentment all over again. There is one old, black-and-white photograph in particular that disturbs me. It sits over the television in the family room, and whenever I look at it, I am filled with conflicting emotions. She died very young, and this photo is one of the few that my family has of her. The picture reveals a strong, young, and happy woman, but to me it exposes her biggest weakness in life and reminds me of the magnitude of my loss.

In the photograph, my mother is sitting upright in a leather chair with a floral dress on. It was her favorite chair in the house, and when I was a little girl, I would curl up in it to smell her scent—lavender mixed with tobacco. Her black hair is so dark it blends into the background, but her eyes sparkle with a mystifying light. Her face is sweetly curved, and I can make out the small mole over her pouty top lip. Resting in the crook of her right arm is my sleeping younger brother, who was about six months old at the time.

As I look at the photograph, my eyes are drawn to the cigarette box that sits on the table next to her and that is when I begin to feel bitter. My mother was a good mother; she always made time for me and my siblings, and she was always helping us with school work, hugging and kissing us, and teaching us how to draw, cook, or ride a bike. All my loving memories of her wilt when I see that cigarette box. She always made time for her cigarettes also. The smell of tobacco was always on her, and a cigarette always at hand.

My mother appears healthy and sweet in this photograph, but shortly thereafter, she died at the age of thirty-three from lung cancer. I was nine when she died, and I did not understand her death; I only knew that she had left my siblings and me without a mother. As much as she had loved us, she loved her tobacco. She should have been strong enough to stop smoking, strong enough to stay with us, and strong enough to love us more than her drug.

Despite the hurt I feel at her leaving us, this photograph captures her as she was before the cancer ravaged her. This photograph of my beautiful, sweet, chain-smoking mother is one of the most precious things my family has. Even though I would much rather have her here with us, this photograph keeps her memory alive in my heart.

1. Consider the introduction. What method is used to "hook" the reader's interest? Does the introduction offer sufficient introductory sentences about the topic? What dominant impression is emphasized?

_____

_____

_____

2. What kind of sensory details are used to convey the dominant impression? Are they sufficient? How are they organized into the supporting paragraphs? What could be improved?

_____

_____

_____

3. Circle the transitional words or expressions. What order (space or time) is used to move the reader from sensory detail to another? What changes might you make?

_____

_____

4. Does the conclusion restate the dominant impression and end with a final observation? How effective is it?

5. What point of view is used in the essay? Is it relevant to the writer's purpose? Is it consistent throughout the essay?

6. Is the title effective? Why or why not?

SUGGESTED TOPICS FOR WRITING DESCRIPTION ESSAYS

Choose one of the following topics or use one of your own and then use prewriting techniques to develop your draft for a description essay.

A retail store
A traditional celebration
A common object like a cell phone, laptop, or blow dryer
Your favorite coworker
Your favorite product or service
A teacher or student
Your favorite spot on campus

BUILDING SKILLS TOGETHER 8-2: Description Essay Feedback Checklist

Once the rough draft of your description essay is completed, have a partner read it and answer the following revision and editing questions. You may also use this checklist to revise and edit your own essay.

Revising Essay Structure

- ☐ Does the introduction capture the attention of the reader? What topic is described? Are there sufficient informational sentences about the topic? What changes might you make?

- ☐ Underline the thesis. Does it include a statement of the topic and a clear dominant impression? What changes might you make?

- ☐ Are clear, specific, and related supporting paragraphs used to convey sensory details about the focused topic? What changes might you make?

- ☐ Is each supporting paragraph sufficiently developed with enough sensory details about the topic? Where can you make improvements?

- ☐ Are clear transition words used to move you through the supporting paragraphs? What order do the transitions show? Where might you make changes?

- ☐ Does the conclusion end the essay's discussion? Does it restate the dominant impression and offer a final observation? What changes might you make?

- ☐ Is the point of view in the essay consistent and relevant? Are any changes needed?

- ☐ How effective is the title in capturing the essay's content? Why or why not?

Editing Spelling, Diction, and Sentence Construction

- ☐ Are there any misspelled words?

- ☐ Are appropriate and specific words used?

- ☐ Are any slang words, text message language, or clichés used?

- ☐ Consider sentence structure and correct any errors with:

  - ☐ Fragments, run-ons, and comma splices
  - ☐ Misplaced or dangling modifiers
  - ☐ Verb tense consistency
  - ☐ Pronoun agreement
  - ☐ Subject and verb agreement

Refer to Appendix A for a review of grammar concepts.

Final Assessment

- ☐ What do you like the most about the essay?

- ☐ What are you unclear about or have difficulty with in the essay?

CHAPTER NINE: Narration
Building Essays with Stories

In television shows, in novels and fairy tales, or in social gatherings, you are entertained by scary, funny, or silly stories. Although you connect with others through that medium, you also share your experiences and your knowledge through storytelling. In some college classes, you may be required to tell stories about any number of subjects, such as perseverance in facing obstacles, heartbreak, historical tragedies, and much more.

A narrative essay is often a storytelling essay designed to share experiences or life lessons. Real or made-up stories can entertain, instruct, clarify, or persuade readers and help them understand and cope with the world. When you write a real or made-up narrative, you focus on a particular experience or situation and make a specific point so you can make it significant for readers to understand something about themselves, about other people, or about the world they live in.

Stories may be told using the **past tense** because they may be experiences that have happened in the past to you or to others. Usually, stories have endings, which signal that they are finished and have happened in the past. As you become more skillful at writing narratives, you may venture beyond the past tense, but for now, writing stories using the past tense is a good place to start. You can tell stories in one of two points of view:

- **First-person narration:** This is when you describe a personal experience using first-person pronouns such as *I* or *we*.
- **Third-person narration:** This is when you describe what happened to someone else, and you use third-person pronouns such as *he, she,* or *they.*

🖐 MEMORY TIP

Point of view identifies from whose perspective the story is told. There are three kinds of points of view, but generally the first- and third-person points of view are most commonly used in narratives.

- **First-person** point of view uses the pronouns *I* or *we*. In a first-person narrative, the story is conveyed by a narrator who is also a character within the story. It is used as a way to communicate directly the internal or unspoken thoughts of the narrator.

- **Second-person** point of view uses the pronouns *you* or *your*. It is the rarest mode in literature or storytelling because the narrator refers to one of the characters as *you*, therefore making the audience member feel as if he or she is a character within the story.

- **Third-person** point of view uses the pronouns *she, he, it, they, him, her*, or *names of people*. Third-person narration provides the greatest flexibility to the author and thus is the most commonly used narrative mode in literature. In a third-person narrative, the narrator does not participate in the action of the story as one of the characters, but lets us know exactly how the characters feel. We learn about the characters through this outside voice.

Refer to Chapter One for a complete explanation of point of view.

WRITING A NARRATION ESSAY

To write a narrative essay, decide on the experience or situation you want to focus on showing and the lesson you want to share with the reader. Sometimes you may not have a clear idea of the lesson you want to share, but write the draft anyway and along the way the lesson will become clearer. At other times, you may know what lesson you want to share, but you may not have an actual story. You can make one up, but whether you make it up or it is real, a good way to learn strong narrative skills is by learning and mastering five elements.

- background
- conflict
- order of events
- outcome
- lesson

These elements make it easier for the writer to build a story with a good beginning, middle, and ending.

> **⬛ MEMORY TIP**
>
> The five elements in a narrative make up the acronym BCOOL (pronounced as be cool):
>
> - **B**ackground
> - **C**onflict
> - **O**rder of events
> - **O**utcome
> - **L**esson
>
> Although BCOOL is not the only way to tell a story, it is one of many effective ways that make it easier for a writer to create a narrative. As you get more practice, you can begin to experiment by putting these elements in different orders or in using only some of the elements.

Using a made-up scenario involving claustrophobia as the topic, consider how these elements help create a narrative:

1. **B**ackground: This should appear in several sentences. This specifies ***where*** and ***when*** the situation happened and ***who*** was or were involved. It is the description of the situation's time, location, and people and may be described briefly or at length.

> Person struggling with claustrophobia or fear of tight spaces.

2. **C**onflict: This is the heart of the narrative. It is *what* the narrative tries to solve. It shows what the problem is. The problem could be one of the following:
   - man vs. man: a person against another person or a group of people.
   - man vs. nature: a person or persons against a force of nature like a blizzard, tornado, starvation.
   - man vs. himself: a person against a fear or insecurity that is inside, like a person who is afraid of heights or commitment.

> Man vs. himself: Ocean diving encloses the claustrophobic diver in a dark, airless water tomb.

3. **O**rder of events: This is the step-by-step sequence of events to show *how* the conflict is being dealt with. This is the longest and most descriptive

part of the narrative. Here is where the details have to be vivid and well-organized, the suspense is built, and dialogue is used.

> First, the character takes diving classes.
> Then, the character manages well in pool classes.
> Eventually, the character panics in the actual dive in 60 feet of ocean.
> Next, she deals with her claustrophobia under water.

4. **Outcome:** This is the solution to the conflict. This may be briefly stated in a few sentences.

> She overcomes her fear of claustrophobia and is successful on her ocean dive.

5. **Lesson:** This answers the "so what" question for the reader. It is the importance of the story: the lesson learned, realized, shown, or shared with the reader. It is the point of telling about the conflict and the outcome. It can be simply stated or implied. It can appear in the topic sentence and be implied or restated in the concluding sentence.

> Addressing a fear is better than living with it all your life.

 BUILDING TIP

1. The use of **description** (imagery of the characters, the places, the objects in the story) and **transitions** (words that help the reader move from idea to idea) are not only required for narrative paragraphs but also mandatory to enhance and enrich your narrative.

2. Sometimes, **dialogue** is used to show the interactions between the story's characters. Dialogue shows the conversations or verbal exchanges between characters. Dialogue must be put inside quotation marks (" ") and follow a conversational tag word such as *said, exclaimed, cried*. Commas follow the conversational tag word and periods at the end of quotations must go inside the second quotation mark.

    Ron turned to Sara and said, "I am glad you joined us on this hike."

    Sara replied, "Something told me I should not miss this adventure."

After you have broken down your story into the five elements, you can write it as an essay. In your essay, do not announce the BCOOL elements like this:

The conflict was ...

The order of events is seen ...

In other words, do not tell the reader your story, but show or reveal your story. To show your story, organize your thoughts based on the BCOOL elements but express them in engaging language that describes the background, conflict, order of events, and outcome.

GENERIC PLAN FOR A NARRATIVE ESSAY

In the body of the essay, you may designate your narrative elements in different paragraphs.

Introduction Paragraph
     Background information
     Thesis = Focused Topic (Experience + Lesson)
Supporting Paragraphs 1 to 3
     Conflict description
     Order of events
     More order of events
     Final order of events and outcome
     Lesson
Conclusion Paragraph
     Restatement of thesis and lesson
     Final observation

Introduction Paragraph

The introduction in a narrative essay gives background information about the place, time, and characters of the experience or story. This should be accomplished before the thesis statement. Try not to divulge the conflict in the introduction; instead, build up the suspense for it.

Thesis Statement

A narrative makes a point about an experience so that the reader is invested in reading it. For example, a story about eavesdropping on an evil conversation is not as interesting as a story about having your integrity tested after hearing that conversation.

The thesis statement includes the experience or story and the lesson learned or realized. The experience is summed up in a few words while the lesson tells what the reader will take from your narrative; it is the answer to the "so what?"

question about your story. To create a meaningful thesis sentence, ask yourself these questions:

- How did I change?
- What did I learn?
- What is important to me about this experience?

Wrong: I volunteer.

Right: A volunteer experience showed me how valuable it is to give to others.

👆 MEMORY TIP

Thesis Statement = Focused Topic (Experience + Lesson)

A diving experience showed me the strength to overcome my claustrophobia.

   ↑   ↑

Experience   *Lesson*

BUILDING SKILLS 9-1: Deciding on a Lesson

Write a main point or lesson you might choose for each topic.

1. Topic: A breakup of a friendship
   Lesson: _____

   _____

2. Topic: An embarrassing experience at a party
   Lesson: _____

   _____

BUILDING SKILLS 9-2: Recognizing Effective Narration Thesis Statements

Put *TS* next to the sentences that are effective narrative thesis statements and *X* next to those that are not.

1. The roach found in my hamburger will be discussed. _____

2. A spouse's betrayal tested my definition of loyalty. _____

3. Mrs. Smith has two cats. _____

4. This essay is about the importance of school. _____

5. Hot dogs are good for barbecues.   _____

6. This is a paper about the effects of pollution.   _____

7. I want to tell you about my first time getting a job.   _____

8. My eighteenth birthday party taught me the value of knowing
   your friends.   _____

9. Taking care of a special needs child has taught me the value
   of sacrifice.   _____

10. My last drink of alcohol was the beginning of a better life
    through better health.   _____

Supporting Paragraphs

The supporting paragraphs show the conflict, order of events, outcome, and lesson. The unfolding of the elements should happen in chronological order within the body paragraphs and build to a climax or peak before the conflict is resolved. Be selective in which events you include because you want to have the ones that most clearly demonstrate your main point or lesson.

The development sentences in narratives come from the vivid details you use to show the story. These details add interest and suspense to the story and help the reader become involved. Be sure to use vivid details and dialogue to enrich your narrative.

In narrative essays, supporting paragraphs and development sentences go hand in hand with transitions, especially time or chronological transitions, because they make the order of events clearer to readers.

TRANSITIONS USED IN NARRATION ESSAYS

after	eventually	meanwhile	soon	earlier
as	finally	next	then	suddenly
at last	first	now	when	by this time
before	last	second	while	as soon as
during	later	since		

Phrases with specific times or dates such as *in 2001. . . after two days . . . at 2 o'clock . . . two minutes later . . .*

Consult Appendix B for a complete list of transitions.

BUILDING SKILLS 9-3: Identifying Support

Read the following essay and, under each appropriate heading that follows, list the supporting details that fit each narrative element.

A routine shift at work taught me the importance of quick action. My shift at the Biscuit Korner is six hours long, and on Wednesdays I close up the diner. Mr. Temple was one of the regular customers, and everyone knew he was the town's longtime widower and kindest man around.

On November 16, 2007, an hour before closing time, Mr. Temple, who had finished his usual dinner for Wednesday, sat staring into his coffee mug while I tidied up and swept up the scraps of food left behind by the other diners. Everyone had left and as the rain beat against the diner's windows, and the wind howled outside, I patiently counted the minutes until closing time. My back hurt, my feet were sore, and I just wanted to be home on such a cold night.

On my way to the kitchen to put the broom away, I glanced at Mr. Temple and noticed that he looked unusually pale and seemed overwhelmingly tired and sad. I decided to sit and chat with him for a while. When I got near him, I noticed that he was very calm. I started talking to him but got no reply, so I leaned down to get his attention. When he lifted his eyes, I noticed they were glazed over, and the left side of his face was twitching. He tried to mouth something to me, but I did not understand him. Fear settled in my heart. I knew something was wrong, but I did not know what it was. I grabbed his arm and started asking him questions. As he tried to look at me again, I saw his eyes roll over in his head and felt his body go limp under my hand. Heavily, he slumped away from me onto the booth's seat. I gasped and thought he must be dead. But no, his chest was still moving! All of a sudden, I felt the silence in the diner as if everything slowed down to a stop right then. Shaking and scared, I quickly went through what I should do and decided I should call for medical help.

I scrambled to the phone and dialed the emergency number. Hysterically, I explained to the kind man on the line where I was and what had happened, and he assured me that help was on the way. I went back to Mr. Temple's side and felt his clammy forehead. He was still breathing, but barely. Helpless, I held his hand and prayed he would be fine.

Thirty seconds later, I heard the ambulance sirens and then the paramedics were there. Scared but relieved, I watched them take over. Five minutes later, they wheeled him out of the diner. Later, they told me he had suffered a stroke, and my quick actions had saved his life. Three weeks later, Mr. Temple came for his usual Wednesday night dinner, and I was so happy to see him alive and well.

From this narrative, list details about:

Background: _____
_____
_____
_____
_____

Conflict: _____
_____
_____
_____
_____

Order of Events: _____
_____
_____
_____
_____

Outcome: _____
_____
_____
_____
_____

Lesson: _____
_____
_____
_____
_____

BUILDING SKILLS 9-4: Completing the BCOOL Pattern

For each topic, complete the last three narrative elements that follow the BCOOL pattern of narrative writing.

1. Topic: Cheating
   Background: During a math test, a student copies from the student next to
                him the answers to two problems.
   Conflict: Two classmates saw the student cheat.

   Order of Events: _____

   _____

   _____

   Outcome: _____

   _____

   _____

   Lesson: _____

   _____

   _____

2. Topic: Embezzled money and honesty
   Background: Ed knows that his fellow employee, Tom, steals money and
                products from the company.
   Conflict: Ed sees Tom taking the money from the register when the
                company owner turns his back.

   Order of Events: _____

   _____

   _____

   Outcome: _____

   _____

   _____

   Lesson: _____

   _____

   _____

Conclusion Paragraph

The objective of the conclusion paragraph is to end the discussion; therefore, offer a thoughtful observation or remark about the lesson you learned from the experience you described. Do not start a new idea, but close off your discussion. Consider the following conclusion for the essay on claustrophobia.

As we concluded our dive, I grasped that my claustrophobia can be controlled. Now, nothing can stop me from discovering the ocean's mysterious depths. In fighting this debilitating anxiety, I have conquered my fear of tight places and have gained a new strength to discover new worlds. I stand ready to dive into my next adventure.

EXAMPLE OF A NARRATION ESSAY

Dive into My Phobia

For as long as I can remember I have been fascinated with the ocean and have longed to explore its shadowy world, but aside from Discovery Channel, the other way to do so is to go diving into its mysterious depths. Sadly, I do not know how to dive, and I am claustrophobic. Ever since fifth grade, I have known that I fear enclosed spaces. Tight spaces always make me panic because I feel too restricted and choked. At the urging of my fiancé, and despite my grave reservations, I agreed to join him on his upcoming ocean dive with the understanding that I had to be taught how to dive first in spite of my severe claustrophobia. How would I be able to overcome this fear that has dogged me all my life? This dive taught me the extent of my resilience.

Eight weeks before the ocean dive and with a deep sense of doom, I enrolled in a diving class and made sure that the diving instructor was aware of my claustrophobia. During the first week of instruction, we hardly touched water and learned mostly about the basics and chemistry of diving. Over the course of the next 3 weeks, we trained in shallow pool water, 3 to 10 feet deep, and all was going well. With each practice session, my claustrophobia was waning, and I was getting more confident and comfortable with the idea and the process. Even the practice dive down to 20 feet of ocean water did not scare me. Then, the big day came for the ocean dive to 60 feet.

As I sat on the ledge of the bobbing boat, a quarter of a mile off the San Diego coast, my stomach was churning with nerves. The dark-blue water beckoned me as I suited up in my diving gear, but my heart was pounding with anticipation and fear. I have worked so hard for this, and I was determined to do it. Ignoring my anxiety, I stepped onto the swim step, put the regulator in my mouth, took a few breaths, and plunged in. Instantly, the water rushed around me, and I was now at the mercy of this new world. I started the descent and equalized the pressure in my ears. My diving instructor swam alongside me. As I continued my descent, my breathing grew deeper and faster, and I began to feel the water pressure on my wetsuit as the water got darker. I did not know how deep I would go but, all of a sudden, panic hit me. Suddenly, everything was closing in on me and that familiar feeling of fear seized me. I felt like I was trapped in a tiny hole with no air or light, and my brain froze. With the echo of my own rapid breathing in my ears, I started thrashing around looking for a way out. A great sense of desperation and doom filled me, and flight was the only thought on my mind, but I did not want to give in anymore, so I resolved to fight the feelings. I closed my eyes and focused on slowing my breathing. I felt my diving instructor grab my shoulder and turn me around. I opened my eyes, we were eye to eye, and I felt better knowing someone was with me. As I stared at him wanting to scream, I saw his hand give me the okay sign and point to his depth gauge to show me we were at 60 feet. At once my brain snapped out of its frozen state, and I registered that I had made it all the way down to my goal. I was still alive! As fast as it came, my overwhelming fear dissolved, and I felt triumphant. I smiled at my instructor, gave him the okay sign, looked around me slowly, and took measure of the beauty of the deep ocean.

As we concluded our dive, I grasped that my claustrophobia can be controlled. Now, nothing can stop me from discovering the ocean's mysterious depths. In fighting this debilitating anxiety, I have conquered my fear of tight places and have gained a new strength to discover new worlds. I stand ready to dive into my next adventure.

BUILDING SKILLS TOGETHER 9-1: Evaluating a Narration Essay

Working in a small group, read the following essay and answer the evaluation questions that follow.

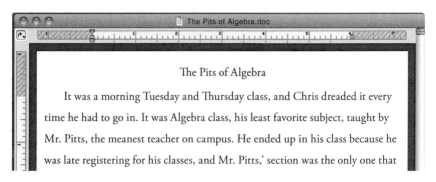

The Pits of Algebra

It was a morning Tuesday and Thursday class, and Chris dreaded it every time he had to go in. It was Algebra class, his least favorite subject, taught by Mr. Pitts, the meanest teacher on campus. He ended up in his class because he was late registering for his classes, and Mr. Pitts,' section was the only one that still had available seats. Although he regretted taking this class, Chris learned the value of perseverance.

Mr. Pitts was a demanding, conceited, and self-absorbed person famous for saying, "If you work hard in this class, you'll pass. If you don't, I promise you nothing." He gave an excessive amount of homework that was complicated and hard to complete. He always lectured quickly with his back to the class and never paused to assess if anyone understood what he had covered. He also gave brain-crushing tests where no student ever scored higher than a 70. By week two of the semester, Chris, the straight A student, was hopelessly lost with the material. He could not make sense of anything when it came to Algebra, and he dared not ask a question in class for fear that Mr. Pitts would slaughter him with sarcasm. No matter how hard he tried, he failed all his tests and was hopelessly discouraged. Sadly, he could not afford to fail this class if he wanted to finish his degree on time, but he did not know what to do about his problem with Mr. Pitts.

After seeking advice from his counselor and his friends, Chris decided to approach Mr. Pitts in his office before class. Chris set up an appointment and went in to see him with a heavy heart. During their ten-minute conversation, Chris learned that Mr. Pitts was not interested in helping him learn Algebra; he was just interested in collecting a paycheck. His opinion of his teacher grew worse, and Chris decided to seek help on his own, so he went to the tutoring center and set up tutoring sessions for the rest of the semester. He also cleared his calendar for the weekends, and resolved to put every ounce of his energy into understanding Algebra.

For four weeks, Chris lived, breathed, and ate Algebra. He studied diligently every night and weekend and religiously kept his tutoring appointments. Algebra was making sense now, and by the time the midterm came around, Chris was ready. The midterm was to count for 50% of the overall course grade. On the day of the midterm, he walked confidently into class and smiled at his teacher who glared back at him. He was the first one to finish and as he turned in his test, he smiled again at Mr. Pitts, who silently snarled at him. At the next class meeting, the students waited with apprehension as the teacher passed back the tests. Chris sat patiently and stoically until Mr. Pitts gave him his. When he saw the A grade on the paper, he double-checked to make sure his name was on it; and then, he whooped for joy. He had done it; he had learned Algebra on his own.

Although Chris would never recommend Mr. Pitts to anyone, he realized that this teacher forced him to learn a valuable lesson in life: When you are down and out, get up and fight; do not give up. Yes, Mr. Pitts was the pits in teaching, but he taught Chris the value of perseverance.

1. Consider the introduction. Does the introduction provide background information on the experience/story? What details describe the background?

_____

_____

_____

2. Underline the thesis statement. Is there a clear thesis statement that identifies the experience and lesson? Is the thesis statement effective? What might you change or add?

_____

_____

_____

3. How many supporting paragraphs are used to develop the thesis? How are they organized?

_____

_____

_____

4. What details describe the conflict?

_____

_____

_____

5. What details describe the order of events?

_____

_____

_____

6. What details describe the outcome?

_____

_____

_____

7. Is there a conclusion paragraph? Does the conclusion provide the lesson learned from the experience? How? Does it end with a final observation? How?

8. What point of view is used in this narrative essay? Is it relevant or effective to the writer's purpose? Is it consistent throughout the essay?

9. Is the title effective? Why or why not?

SUGGESTED TOPICS FOR WRITING NARRATION ESSAYS

Choose one of the following topics or use one of your own and then use prewriting techniques to develop your draft for a narration essay.

Accepting a dare that led to trouble
A disastrous date
An ethical dilemma involving a coworker or subordinate
A rebellious act
An occasion when you experienced rejection
A time when you witnessed or displayed courage

Pick a saying as the lesson of your narrative:

Borrowing is the mother of trouble.

If it is not broken, do not fix it.

It is not what you know; it is who you know.

Haste makes waste.

❚ BUILDING TOGETHER 9-2: Narrative Essay
❚ Feedback Checklist

Once the rough draft of your narration essay is completed, have a partner read it and answer the following revision and editing questions. You may also use this checklist to revise and edit your own essay.

Revising Essay Structure

☐ Does the introduction capture the attention of the reader? Are sufficient introductory sentences provided about the background for this experience? What changes might you make?

☐ Underline the thesis. Does it indicate the experience and lesson that the essay is focused on? What changes might you make?

☐ Consider the sentences that describe the background. Are there enough details about the background? What changes might you make?

☐ Consider the sentences that present the conflict. What is the conflict? What changes might you make?

☐ Is the order of events logical? What changes might you make?

☐ What is the outcome? Was the result an effective solution to the conflict? How so? What changes might you make?

☐ Consider the sentences that provide the meaning or lesson to the narrative. Do you think the meaning or significance of this narrative is strong and relevant? What changes might you make?

☐ Are clear transition words used to move you through the order of events? Where might you make changes?

☐ Does the conclusion paragraph close with a thoughtful remark and remind the reader of the experience and lesson? What changes might you make?

☐ Is the point of view in the essay consistent and relevant? Are any changes needed?

☐ How effective is the title in capturing the essay's content? Why or why not?

Editing Spelling, Diction, and Sentence Construction

☐ Are there any misspelled words?

☐ Are appropriate and specific words used?

☐ Are any slang words, text message language, or clichés used?

☐ Consider sentence structure and correct any errors with:

    ☐ Fragments, run-ons, and comma splices

    ☐ Misplaced or dangling modifiers

    ☐ Verb tense consistency

    ☐ Pronoun agreement

    ☐ Subject and verb agreement

Refer to Appendix A for a review of grammar concepts.

Final Assessment

☐ What do you like the most about the essay?

☐ What are you unclear about or have difficulty with in the essay?

CHAPTER TEN: Definition
Building Essays with Clarifications

You might say that your grandmother is *frugal,* that your local library is *cozy,* or that your house is *shabby.* Without some explanation, these italicized terms mean very little. To make your meaning clear, you should define what you mean by *frugal, cozy,* or *shabby.* Some college assignments may involve the use of definition; for example, in a chemistry class, you may be asked to define *alkalinity;* in a business class, you may be asked to define *consumer confidence;* in a philosophy class, you may be asked to define *existentialism.*

To **define** means to give the meaning of words. The word *definition* leads many people to think of a dictionary, but defining involves more than looking up the meaning of a word. It involves two kinds of meaning or definitions: denotation and connotation.

Denotation is the most specific and actual meaning for a word—often found in a dictionary.

In the dictionary, the word *alien* is defined as "a being from another planet."

Connotation is the implied suggested meaning for a word—not necessarily found in a dictionary.

Connotations for the word *alien* include such notions as "strange, unfamiliar, or foreign."

Definition essays involve writing that explains what something means. As a starting point for writing definition essays, you may consult the dictionary for the formal meaning or the **denotation** of the term and then consider your own personal interpretation of the term. In your essay, develop and show your own definition of the term—your own **connotation.**

WRITING A DEFINITION ESSAY

When you write a definition essay, you need to understand the term you are using before you can define it for others. Start by reading the dictionary's definition of your term and prewriting ideas about its meaning. Then, explain the term in your own words. A good strategy to follow is:

1. Decide on the term you want to define and read its dictionary definition.
2. Develop your own personal definition for the term using one of the following ways:
   - **Definition by synonym:** Use a word that means the same thing as your term.
     Success means achievement.
   - **Definition by negation:** Explain what the term is not.
     Success is *not* the amount of money one has.
   - **Definition by category:** Compare the term to other members of its class and then show the differences. These differences are special characteristics that make the term stand out. Defining by category has two parts: the general class the word belongs to and the way the word is distinguished or distinctive from other words in that class. For example, lung is in the category of organ, but it is different from the other organs like brain, heart, liver, and so on because it pumps oxygen into the bloodstream. Consider this example:

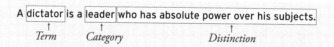

A dictator is a leader who has absolute power over his subjects.
↑   ↑   ↑
Term   *Category*   *Distinction*

3. Decide how you will organize your explanation of the definition. Definition essays do not follow any one particular pattern of development. In fact, a definition essay may explain the definition of a term using any of the previous patterns discussed in this text.

⚒ BUILDING TIP

Definition essays do not follow any one specific pattern of development; instead, they use any of the writing patterns discussed in previous chapters (illustration, cause or effect, comparison or contrast, narration, or description). Often, description essays use a **combination of patterns**; for example, a definition essay may define the term *success* and make a point about it by giving examples and narrating a story.

To decide on a pattern of organization, reflect on the best pattern or patterns that help you show or explain your term. You may want to refer to the previous chapters about the different writing patterns. Some patterns will be more useful for particular terms, so use the pattern that best suits your purpose.

Suppose you use the word *stereotype* for a working definition essay. According to Webster's *New World Dictionary*, the term *stereotype* means "a fixed notion or conception of a person, group, idea, etc., held by a number of people and allowing for no individuality or critical judgment." Approach the definition essay by identifying your connotative definition of the term and by deciding on the writing pattern to use in organizing your explanation of the definition. Consider this prewrite of all the possible writing patterns for stereotypes.

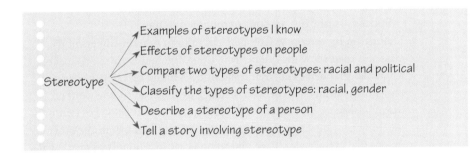

Which pattern seems most interesting to you? Pick that one and use it as the organizing pattern for your supporting paragraphs and development sentences. Once you have decided on the definition and on the writing pattern or patterns you would like to use, you can start writing a rough draft.

GENERIC PLAN FOR A DEFINITION ESSAY

Introduction Paragraph
    Thesis = Focused Topic (your own definition of the term)
Support Paragraphs and Development Sentences: organized based on selected writing pattern or patterns
Conclusion Paragraph
        Restatement of definition
        Final observation

BUILDING SKILLS 10-1: Recognizing Types of Definitions

Determine the type of each definition. For synonym, write *S* next to the sentence; for negation, write *N*; and for category, write *C*.

1. An oasis is a place of water in the middle of the desert. _____

2. A wife is not a slave. _____

3. Dishonesty is at the root of evil things. _____

4. A wife-beater is a type of sleeveless undershirt worn by men. _____

5. Fame is not happiness. _____

6. Philanthropy is charity. _____

7. Communism is a form of government in which total power is in the hands of the government. _____

8. Ageism is discrimination. _____

9. Pride is a feeling of satisfaction from something accomplished. _____

10. Hope is not despair. _____

Introduction Paragraph

In the introduction, you may offer several general sentences about the term or topic. You may show the history of things related to the term, or the term's effect on society or on a group of people, or on a process, and so on.

Thesis Statement

The thesis statement in a definition essay shows the writer's intentions for the definition. In other words, what point is the writer trying to demonstrate about the term? The thesis statement includes the term and your definition of the term. Your definition is the way you view that term, so for a definition essay about the term *stereotype*, you can state your definition in one of several ways: by synonym, by negation, or by category.

 **BUILDING TIP**

Thesis Statement by Synonym = Term + means/is + definition

> A stereotype is a <u>label</u>.

Thesis Statement by Negation = Term + is not + definition

> A stereotype is <u>not a positive classification</u>.

Thesis Statement by Category = Term + is + category + definition.

> A stereotype is a <u>fixed conception that negatively marks or brands people or things</u>.

Whichever way you decide to state your definition, be sure to use the words *means* and *is* in your thesis statement and avoid troublesome phrases like *is when* or *is where*. A common practice is to define the noun with a noun, the adjective with an adjective and so on.

> ## ⚒ BUILDING TIP
>
> It is good practice to avoid the use of the *is when* or *is where* expressions in your thesis statement because these adverb phrases limit your definition and imply that your term can only hold true in specific conditions.
>
> **Depression is when one is not happy.**
>
> This sentence implies that whenever a person is unhappy, that person is depressed. What about those who are not happy because they are sick with the flu?

BUILDING SKILLS 10-2: Recognizing Effective Definition Thesis Statements

Write *TS* next to the sentences that are effective definition thesis statements and *X* next to those that are not.

1. Several historical events demonstrate the impact of democracies or governments based on majority decision making. _____

2. Generosity is when someone gives too much. _____

3. Alternative Rock is my favorite style of music. _____

4. Overachievers are workaholics who create several effects on people around them. _____

5. Racism or prejudice against other races in our society is apparent in several ways. _____

6. Several events in my life have shown me how education is inspiration. _____

7. Monogamy is where someone is married to only one person at a time. _____

8. In today's society, the word *communication* means Internet network sites such as Twitter and Facebook. _____

9. Fifteen minutes of fame is when someone is in the limelight. _____

10. My sister's life is centered around her being a socialite or a trendsetter. _____

BUILDING SKILLS 10-3: Writing Definition Thesis Statements

Use the prewriting technique demonstrated here to determine the development pattern (illustration, cause/effect, compare/contrast, narration, or description) you would choose for the terms listed. Then write a thesis statement for the term that indicates your chosen pattern.

Hero
- Examples of real or imaginary heroes I know
- Effects of real or imaginary heroes on our youth
- Compare two heroes I know: my father and my father-in-law
- Classify three kinds of heroes based on the types of accomplishments
- Describe a person I regard as a hero
- Tell a story of a hero I witnessed in action

1. Term to be defined: Obstacles

   Pattern for definition:

   _____

   Thesis statement:

   _____

2. Term to be defined: Gambling

   Pattern for definition:

   _____

   Thesis statement:

   _____

3. Term to be defined: Traditions
   Pattern for definition:

   _____

   Thesis statement:

   _____

4. Term to be defined: Responsibility
   Pattern for definition:

   _____

   Thesis statement:

   _____

5. Term to be defined: Self-respect
   Pattern for definition:

   _____

   Thesis statement:

   _____

Supporting Paragraphs

The supporting paragraphs in a definition essay are the examples, explanations, and facts that clarify your term. Their content and structure depends on the writing pattern you select to use. You may use illustration, description, cause or effect, comparison or contrast, narration, or a combination of a few to develop your definition essay. Some patterns will be more useful for particular terms. Use the pattern that best suits your purpose. Consider this a prewrite that indicates possible writing patterns for stereotypes.

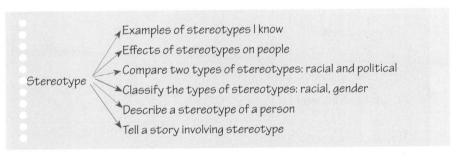

Pick one and use it as the organizing pattern for your supporting paragraphs and development sentences. Suppose you consider examples (illustration) as a writing pattern for an essay on stereotype.

TRANSITIONS USED IN DEFINITION ESSAYS

The transitions you use depend on the pattern of writing you are using for supporting paragraphs and development sentences. Consult the individual chapters of the writing patterns or the complete guide to transitions in Appendix B.

In keeping with the example of illustration as the organizing pattern for a stereotype essay, use the transitions that correspond with that writing pattern: *first example, another example,* and *most important example.*

Conclusion Paragraph

The objective of the conclusion paragraph is to end the discussion; therefore, refer to the chapter that corresponds to the pattern(s) you have chosen to develop your definition and follow the concluding process for each pattern. Generally, though, you may offer a thoughtful observation or remark about the topic, being mindful to restate your supporting ideas and thesis statement.

If illustration is used in a definition essay, the conclusion paragraph usually repeats the supporting examples as they were presented in the essay and provide a final observation. Consider this example of a conclusion for an essay on stereotype.

The jocks, the nerds, and the preps are examples of stereotypes of high school students. High school is a perfect microcosm of what happens in the big world, and if our students are learning and using these stereotypes at that point in their lives, is it any wonder we have a dysfunctional society based on peer pressure and self-image? In the end, the preconceived ideas we have about others blind us to their reality and prevent us from taking the trouble to learn what others are really like.

EXAMPLE OF A DEFINITION ESSAY
Method of Organization: Illustration

Distorted Notions

Stereotyping is widespread in our society and involves the overgeneralization of the reality of a person, concept, or idea. The motive behind it is to enhance one's own identity in one's mind. Unfortunately, it is the foundation for prejudice and discrimination, and it prevents one from getting to know others as they are. These biased notions are learned at a young age from parents, other family members, educators, peers, media, etc. Even positive stereotypes, like negative stereotypes, are harmful to those they target because they affect one's self-image and add pressure to conform. A stereotype is a preconceived notion or idea that brands or marks others. Based on their interests in school, there are several examples of stereotyped high school students.

A common stereotype of high school students is the jocks. Jocks are the athletes who live and breathe sports; they know what team has the most points, touchdowns, and RBIs. They are perceived as single-minded, popular, and as partiers. They are disliked because often they may receive special treatment from staff members. The teachers may tend to be lenient on grading them and on excusing their absences. Even though many lack scholastic strength, they are able to get scholarships based on their athletic ability. Often, they get letters of acceptance into universities and colleges based mostly on their athletic abilities.

Another stereotype of high school students is the nerds. They are the smart students who exceed the average in intelligence. They are the ones that all jocks come to if they need help passing a test. These kids have 4.0 GPAs; on the other hand, they do not care what others think of them. Most are shy, but they are always willing to help. Although they would like to be popular, they are more interested in being smart.

The most disturbing stereotype of high school students is the divas. They are the pampered princesses. They care about the outer appearance of people. They have average test scores, and they try to use their looks to get what they want. Some of them go around putting people down or making them feel lousy. These kids always have the latest fashion and newest hairstyles. Sometimes they make up their own words that do not make any sense at all. In addition, they judge others based on the clothing they wear or the name brand, the style, and the cost.

The jocks, the nerds, and the divas are examples of stereotypes of high school students. High school is a small-scale version of what happens in the big world, and if our students are learning and using these stereotypes at that point in their lives, is it any wonder we have a society based on peer pressure and self-image? In the end, the preconceived ideas we have about others blind us to their reality and prevent us from taking the trouble to learn what others are really like.

❦ BUILDING SKILLS TOGETHER 10-1: Evaluating a Definition Essay

Working in a small group, read the following essay and answer the evaluation questions that follow.

Sugar and Spice Kitchen.doc

Kindly Speak the Truth

As I was growing up, I watched how my mother dealt with situations. My mother always felt that the easiest way out of any given situation meant telling a "little white lie." When I would come to her with a concern or question about what I should do, she generally advised me to lie. At first I did what she told me: tell lies. Eventually, I learned that honesty means more than not telling lies; it means speaking the truth kindly.

I started thinking of all the "little white lies" I had heard her tell. I remembered the time she told someone that our phone lines had been down when she was trying to explain why she had not been in touch with a friend of hers. Or the time she told Dad that she loved the necklace he gave her for her birthday before she pawned it the very next day. And all the times she included me in her lies, such as the time she told my teacher that I had to miss school for foot surgery when she really needed me to help her clean the house for a party she was giving. It bothered me the most when she would ask me to tell whoever called for her that she was not there when she was.

I was not blessed with her lack of conscience because on many painful occasions I learned that it is worse to be caught in a lie than it is to tell the truth in the first place. On one occasion, I went to my mother for advice; "Mom, I told Yvonne that I would go over to her house after school today, but I would rather go shopping with you." "Tell Yvonne you're sick with fever," she advised, and I did, but Yvonne found out I had told her a lie when she ran into my mother and me at the mall. I felt mortified! I wondered how it was possible that my mother had never learned that lesson.

So, I resolved to teach my mother that honesty is important and involves more than not telling lies. I told her I had decided that it was wrong to tell lies, so when I answered the phone for my mother, I would say, "Lisa, my mother is here, but she does not want to talk to you." She grounded me the first time I did it, but I refused to back down or apologize. I did this four times before she finally understood. She came to me and admitted that her idea of honesty is not right, and I compromised and agreed that mine is a bit too severe. We talked it over and decided that the best thing to do is to find a way to be honest without being rude.

Over the last year, we have worked together to be honest, and we have both reached a point where we speak the truth in kindness. Honesty has come to mean more than not telling lies, and ironically, after I started trying to teach my mom about the meaning of honesty, I ended up getting a better understanding about kindly speaking the truth. In the end, honesty is the best policy.

1. Consider the introduction. What method is used to "hook" the reader's interest?

   _____

   _____

   _____

2. Underline the thesis statement. Does the thesis clearly state a definition without the "is when" or "is where" statements?

   _____

   _____

   _____

3. Is the term defined by the synonym, by negation, or by category?

   _____

   _____

   _____

4. What pattern of writing (illustration, cause or effect, comparison or contrast, description, or narration) is used to support and develop the definition?

   _____

   _____

   _____

5. Circle the transition words or expressions. Are they effective in moving you through the supporting paragraphs? List them and determine the order they show.

6. Is there a conclusion paragraph? How does it end the essay's discussion? What method(s) (restating, observing, remarking, or summarizing) is used to conclude? Explain your answer.

7. What point of view is used in the essay? Is it relevant to the writer's purpose? Is it consistent throughout the essay?

8. Is the title effective? Why or why not?

SUGGESTED TOPICS FOR WRITING DEFINITION ESSAYS

Choose one of the following topics or use one of your own and then use prewriting techniques to develop your draft for a definition essay.

Perseverance	Inspiration
Success	Loyalty
Information overload	Distracted driving
Greed	Courage
Fairness	Self-respect
Customer service	Glass ceiling
Total quality management	Knowledge

♦ BUILDING SKILLS TOGETHER 10-2: Definition
▌ Essay Feedback Checklist

Once the rough draft of your definition essay is completed, have a partner read it and answer the following revision and editing questions. You may also use this checklist to revise and edit your own essay.

Revising Essay Structure

☐ Does the introduction capture the attention of the reader? How do the introductory sentences help the reader understand the term being defined? Are there sufficient introductory sentences before the thesis statement? What changes might you make?

☐ Underline the thesis. Does it include a definition of the term and an indication of the writing pattern being used? What changes might you make?

☐ Are clear, specific, and related supporting paragraphs provided? What changes might you make?

☐ Is each supporting paragraph sufficiently developed with enough development sentences (or FRIEDs)? Where can you make improvements?

☐ Are clear transition words used to move you through the body paragraphs? What order (time, space, importance) do they show? Where might you make changes?

☐ Does the conclusion end the essay's discussion? What concluding method (restating, observing, remarking, or summarizing) is used? What changes might you make?

☐ Is the point of view in the essay consistent and relevant? Are any changes needed?

☐ How effective is the title in capturing the essay's content? Why or why not?

Editing Spelling, Diction, and Sentence Construction

☐ Are there any misspelled words?

☐ Are appropriate and specific words used?

☐ Are any slang words, text message language, or clichés used?

☐ Consider sentence structure and correct any errors with:

  ☐ Fragments, run-ons, and comma splices

  ☐ Misplaced or dangling modifiers

☐ Verb tense consistency

☐ Pronoun agreement

☐ Subject and verb agreement

Refer to Appendix A for a review of grammar concepts.

Final Assessment

☐ What do you like the most about the essay?

☐ What are you unclear about or have difficulty with in the essay?

CHAPTER ELEVEN Literary Analysis
Building Essays about Literature

Sometimes, we learn from each other through narratives or stories. Most movies are created based on stories—written or otherwise. Literature shares stories through novels, short stories, poetry, or drama. Reading literature engages your thinking skills and extends your writing skills into a new dimension of experience. In advanced composition classes, literature classes, or other humanities classes, you may be asked to analyze the literature you have read.

Literary analysis is used to write essays about works of literature. **Literature** consists of works of imagination like poems, short stories, novels, and plays. For example, Shakespeare's *Romeo and Juliet* is a work of literature. Literature allows us to see other people's visions of the world and to indulge in interpreting those visions. Since each person is different in his or her experiences, values, and beliefs, everyone interprets works of literature differently. Literary analysis breaks a work into its parts and allows you to concentrate on the parts you want to use to support your interpretation. It does not retell the story.

WRITING A LITERARY ANALYSIS ESSAY

Writing about literature requires the use of technical terms, and it is helpful to understand what these literary terms and elements are or mean:

- **Theme:** The major issue and what is learned about it in terms of human nature. For example, in *Romeo and Juliet* the main theme is powerful love.
- **Setting:** The time and place of the work. Sometimes it is not important to the story, but other times it might reinforce the theme.
- **Characters:** Individuals appearing in the story. The main character or hero is called the *protagonist*, whereas the character who works against the hero is called the *antagonist*.

- **Plot:** The events that occur in the work or the beginning, middle, and end of a story.
- **Conflict:** The struggle or problem, and it could be between individuals, an individual and society, or something within a character.
- **Climax:** An event signaling a turning point like when the conflict reaches its highest intensity.
- **Point of View:** The perspective from which the story is told. That perspective could be
  - ☐ First person, as in the narrator or central character, and the pronoun *I* is used.
  - ☐ Third person, as in a detached view, and the pronoun *he* or *she* is used.
- **Foreshadowing:** Clues or hints of actions to follow like grey clouds in the sky foreshadow an impending tragic or negative event.
- **Flashback:** A scene that returns to earlier events to clarify the present.
- **Allusion:** Reference to a famous historical event or figure like biblical events or characters.
- **Irony:** The difference between expected and actual elements in the story.
- **Symbol:** Something or someone that represents something larger than itself. For example, a lion in a story symbolizes courage, or a cross represents Christ.

An effective approach to literary analysis is to mark and understand the text. To do so, read the work several times, being sure to annotate or mark it by underlining significant details or writing comments in the margins.

✂ BUILDING TIP

For help analyzing literary works, answer the following questions; then, select, as your focus, the answer that interests you most.

1. What is the setting of the work? Is it important to the work or not?

2. Who are the characters, and what actions motivate the protagonist and the antagonist?

3. How is the plot developed? What is the conflict? Is there foreshadowing?

4. Are symbols used? What are they and what do they mean?

5. Who is the narrator? Is the story told from the first or third person? What impact does that have on your view of the work?

6. What seems to be the theme or message from the work? Is there a social or political statement being made?

7. What lasting impression does the work have on you? What is the most significant element of the work: a scene, a symbol, a character, the theme?

Once you have a focus, start thinking about the elements to use to support your focus. Consider Flannery O'Connor's *A Good Man Is Hard to Find*. This story is about The Misfit, a serial killer who escapes from the Federal Penitentiary and murders an entire family by the side of the road. The family was on its way to a vacation in Tennessee.

GENERIC PLAN FOR A LITERARY ANALYSIS ESSAY

Introduction Paragraph
    Lead
    Author and Title
    Brief plot summary
    Thesis = Focused Topic (Opinion about the Work + Literary Elements)
Supporting Paragraph 1: Topic Sentence 1
    Opening information on quotes
    Quotation
    Explanation
Supporting Paragraph 2: Topic Sentence 2
    Opening information on quotes
    Quotation
    Explanation
Supporting Paragraph 3: Topic Sentence 3
    Opening information on quotes
    Quotation
    Explanation
Conclusion Paragraph
    Repeat the literary elements
    Memorable impression/final observation
Note: A literary analysis essay is always written in the present tense.

Introduction Paragraph

Start your introduction with a strong lead, a hook, or a question related to the theme or character, a relevant quotation from the work, or a general response to the work. Then, identify the author's name and title of the work, and in a few sentences provide a brief plot summary of the work (no more than four sentences). Last, state your thesis statement. Using O'Connor's story, you could focus on The Misfit's character.

> What turns a man into a murderer? Would prison time rehabilitate a man, or would it make him even more wicked? — *Lead*
>
> Flannery O'Connor's "A Good Man is Hard to Find" may provide the answers to these questions. — *Author and title of work*
>
> The Misfit escaped from prison where he was serving his sentence for killing his father. He encounters a family of six on a lonely road in Georgia. They had had a car accident before he happened upon them. For no apparent reason, he has his two helpers kill Bailey, his wife, and their three children, and then he kills the grandmother by shooting her three times in the chest. — *Plot summary*
>
> Undoubtedly, The Misfit is a foul and twisted personality resulting from his disturbing relationship with his father, his time in prison, and his uncertainty over religion. — *Thesis*

Thesis Statement

The thesis statement in a literary analysis essay clearly shows your opinion of the work and the elements you want to show or support in your essay. The thesis statement usually focuses on:

- Several main elements about the story like meaning, structure, or style.
- Several things about **one** element, like the author's use of symbols—explain several examples of symbols used by the author.
- a forecast or list of the important supporting points you intend to use in the body paragraphs.

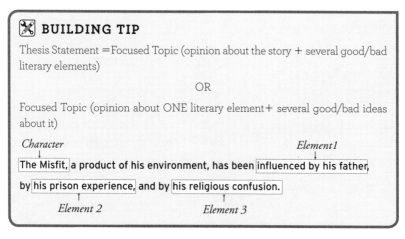

> ✂ **BUILDING TIP**
>
> Thesis Statement = Focused Topic (opinion about the story + several good/bad literary elements)
>
> OR
>
> Focused Topic (opinion about ONE literary element + several good/bad ideas about it)
>
> *Character*   *Element 1*
>
> The Misfit, a product of his environment, has been influenced by his father,
>
> by his prison experience, and by his religious confusion.
>
>   *Element 2*   *Element 3*

BUILDING SKILLS 11-1: Recognizing Effective Literary Analysis Thesis Statements

Write *TS* next to the sentences that are effective literary analysis thesis statements and *X* next to those that are not.

1. I like *The Storm* by Kate Chopin.   _____

2. Ernest Hemingway's *Hills Like White Elephants* shows
   the importance of setting, symbolism, and point of view.   _____

3. Irwin Shaw's *The Girls in Their Summer Dresses* is about a
   womanizing husband.   _____

4. *The Cathedral* by Raymond Carver is effective in its use
   of symbolism and imagery.   _____

5. Edgar Allen Poe's *The Cask of Amontillado* is an interesting
   piece of literature.   _____

6. Sandra Cisneros' *The House on Mango Street* portrays the
   theme of self-identity.   _____

7. Although I did not enjoy William Faulkner's *A Rose for Emily*,
   I will share my feelings about it.   _____

8. *The Use of Force* by William Carlos Williams is effective in its
   use of point of view, character portrayal, and plot sequencing.   _____

9. *The Lesson* by Toni Cade Bambara effectively illustrates the
   devices of voice and style in literary texts.   _____

10. Bessie Head's *The Collector of Treasures* revolves around many
    themes.   _____

Supporting Paragraphs

Each supporting paragraph should include a topic sentence that relates to one of the elements about the story that you stated in your thesis statement. In the topic sentence, for each element repeat the key words from the thesis; then explain your idea and use evidence from the work to prove it. Consider this example of topic sentences for each of the supporting paragraphs in the essay about O'Connor's story.

> I. The Misfit's personality has been shaped by his relationship with his father.
>   Development and Quotation(s) for support

II. The Misfit's prison experience has also had a negative influence on his attitude toward life.

    Development and Quotation(s) for support

III. Confusion over religion is the major cause of The Misfit's distorted personality.

    Development and Quotation(s) for support

Development Sentences

Development sentences in a literary analysis essay consist of textual evidence taken from the work itself, and they involve quotations, explanations, summarizing, and paraphrasing.

⚒ BUILDING TIP

- **Quotations** involve using the author's exact words as they appear in the original text including all punctuation. You use quotations marks (" ") around the quoted material.

- **Paraphrasing** is using your own words to restate the main ideas of a source. You use this when you want detailed information from the original text but not the author's actual words. It is good for breaking down complex discussion.

- **Summarizing** is using your own words to provide a general restatement of the main idea of a text. A summary is always much shorter than the original text.

Refer to Chapter Twelve for a full explanation on citing sources for quotations, paraphrasing, or summarizing.

To be effective at using quotations, paraphrases, and summaries, consider using the following steps:

1. Reread the original text until you understand its full meaning.
2. Highlight or mark possible quotations or sections you may use in your essay.
3. Look at your highlighted or marked sections and decide which ones you will use for quotations or for paraphrasing or summarizing.
4. On note cards, jot down your quotations, being sure to record the source and page number for the quotation on your note card so that you can credit it easily if you decide to use it in your essay.
5. On more note cards, paraphrase or summarize the other sections you have marked, being careful to record the source and page number for future use.
6. Check your version with the original to ensure that your paraphrased or summarized version communicates all the important information.

7. Careful attention to the rules of documentation is important to help you avoid **plagiarism** or the unacknowledged used of other people's words or ideas. You plagiarize when you omit using quotation marks for ideas copied from an original text or when you do not give credit for a paraphrase or summary.

✂ BUILDING TIP

Quotations can be distracting to readers, so use them only when you think they would add strong support to your essay and you feel that the original wording is essential to supporting your thesis. Use quotations when the words from the source would be memorable, would be authoritative, or when paraphrasing or summarizing would change the meaning of the original text's words or phrases.

When you include quotations as part of your supporting paragraphs, provide a brief introduction to the quotation. Once you have stated your quotation, clarify it to show how it proves your topic sentence. The quotation does not need to be lengthy, but it should contain details that you can expand upon and explain to show how and why it supports your topic sentence. Refer to Appendix C: Quotation Protocol to learn how to use quotations.

In the sentences that follow the quotation, comment on, explain, summarize, or paraphrase the meaning, importance, and relevance of the quotation you have chosen to show how and why it fits with your overall thesis statement. Do not assume that the quotation alone is enough to prove your point; you need the explanation (the why and how) part, too. This pattern can be used to include multiple quotations for each topic sentence. Here is a visual representation of the elements needed as developmental sentences in a paragraph that uses multiple quotations as evidence.

Topic Sentence
—Introductory information for quotation
—Quotation
—Explanation and Analysis

—Introductory information for quotation
—Quotation
—Explanation and Analysis

 MEMORY TIP

To make it easier to remember development sentences of supporting paragraphs in a literary analysis essay, use the acronym **QESP** (quotation, explanation, summarizing, or paraphrasing).

Every quotation you use should be followed by a few sentences to summarize, explain, or paraphrase it for the reader, and so that a connection is made between the quotation and the supporting paragraph's topic sentence.

Consider the example below of a fully developed supporting paragraph for O'Connor's story.

The Misfit's adulthood was marked by disturbing feelings about his father. The grandmother suggests that he "must come from nice people," and The Misfit responds, "My Daddy's heart was pure gold," but later he adds, "His father never got in trouble with the Authorities. . . Just had the knack of handling them." *— Quotation*

Later, he claims that his father was a good man who was always clever in how he escaped punishment for his evil actions. *— Paraphrase*

This shows that The Misfit saw his father's flaws and justifies his feelings of anger at the father's opinion of him. *— Explanation*

The Misfit says, "My Daddy said I was a different breed of dog from my brothers and sisters." *— Quotation*

This could have affected The Misfit's self-worth, and he decides to live out his life like his father said as a "different breed." He got into a lot of trouble, which caused tension with his father and resulted in The Misfit murdering him.

He had conflicted feelings towards his father: he hated him and he loved him. He shows the same type of divergent behavior with his victims as he apologizes while cruelly murdering them. *— Explanation and summary*

TRANSITIONS USED IN LITERARY ANALYSIS ESSAYS

one part	first part	one element	area
another part	second part	another element	category
last part	third part	final element	section

Conclusion Paragraph

The conclusion paragraph in a literary analysis essay includes:

- Creative rewording of the thesis and brief summary and emphasis of the importance of each supporting paragraph you included.
- A memorable impression that is a quote from the work or the title of the work used as a final sentence.

Here is how the conclusion might look for the O'Connor story topic:

> Therefore, The Misfit became like his father, capable of both good and evil; but unlike his father, he eliminates the source of confusion in his life by killing his own father. He regards his punishment in prison as cruel as he is unaware of his crime, so to retaliate, he commits more crime. He may have had a belief in religion, but his need for proof of Jesus' deeds damages his faith and leaves him hopeless and angry. There truly is "no real pleasure in life" for the twisted and evil Misfit.

Title

Your title should relate directly to the thesis and the supporting paragraphs. You may use it as your final sentence in the conclusion. The example of O'Connor's story uses a main reference to The Misfit's character and focuses on what created his evil and wicked personality. Consider this example of a title for that essay:

> The Misfit's Twisted Character

EXAMPLE OF A LITERARY ANALYSIS ESSAY

The Misfit's Twisted Character

What turns a man into a murderer? Would prison time rehabilitate a man, or would it make him even more wicked? Flannery O'Connor's "A Good Man Is Hard to Find" may provide the answers to these questions. The Misfit escaped from prison where he was serving his sentence for killing his father. He encounters a family of six on a lonely road in Georgia. They'd had a car accident before he happened upon them. For no apparent reason, he has his two helpers kill Bailey, his wife, and their three children, and then he kills the grandmother by shooting her three times in the chest. Undoubtedly, The Misfit is a foul and twisted personality resulting from his disturbing relationship with his father, his time in prison, and his uncertainty over religion.

The Misfit's adulthood is marked by disturbing feelings about his father. The grandmother suggests that he "must come from nice people," and The Misfit responds, "God never made a finer woman than my mother and my Daddy's heart was pure gold," but later he adds that his father "never got in trouble with the Authorities . . . Just had the knack of handling them." Later, he claims that his father was a good man who was always clever in how he escaped punishment for his evil actions. This shows that The Misfit sees his father's flaws and is angry at his father's treatment and opinions of him. The Misfit says, "My Daddy said I was a different breed of dog from my brothers and sisters." This affects The Misfit's self-worth, and he decides to live out his life like his father said, as a "different breed." He got into a lot of trouble and caused tension with his father which led to The Misfit murdering his father. He had conflicted feelings toward his father: he hated him and he loved him. He shows the same type of divergent behavior with his victims as he apologizes while cruelly murdering them.

The Misfit's prison experience also had a negative influence on his attitude toward life. When the grandmother asks him what he did to go to prison, he answers, "I set there and set there, trying to remember what it was I done and I ain't recalled it to this day . . . I found out the crime don't matter . . . because sooner or later you're going to forget what it was you done and just be punished for it." His view of his time in prison indicates that he is angry at being punished for a crime he doesn't remember or that he doesn't consider a punishable crime. As a result, he feels abused. The Misfit is very clear about his negative experience in prison when he says, "I was buried alive .. .ain't been treated right . . . . " He views his imprisonment as excessive and harsh and wants to treat others like he was treated. He turns to killing innocent people to show that he can be excessive and cruel like society is to him.

Confusion over religion is the major cause of The Misfit's distorted personality. The grandmother asks The Misfit if he ever prays for help from Jesus, and he responds, "I don't want no hep . . . I can't make what all I done wrong fit what all I gone through in punishment." His view is that, like Jesus' crucifixion, he is punished for something he did not do, and he cannot change that. Of course, he chooses not to remember his crime of patricide. Furthermore, Jesus cannot help him because if he believed in Him, he would be punished again spiritually because killing is a sin in the Christian faith. But he also questions his belief in Jesus when he claims that he is not sure if Jesus is all powerful and had raised the dead, " . . . and if He didn't, then it's nothing for you to do but enjoy the few minutes you got left the best way you can—by killing somebody." He wants proof that Jesus did these incredible impossible deeds like raising the dead, and since he doesn't have the proof, he will not believe in Him and therefore there is no reason to be a good, God-fearing person. For him, it is more enjoyable to be evil and mean to others.

Therefore, The Misfit's twisted personality is developed by disturbing forces from his past experiences. He becomes, like his father, capable of both good and evil, but unlike his father, he does not escape punishment. He regards his punishment in prison as cruel and retaliates by committing more evil crime. He may have had a belief in religion, but his need for proof of Jesus' deeds damages his faith and leaves him hopeless and angry. There truly is "no real pleasure in life" for the twisted and evil Misfit.

SUGGESTED TOPICS FOR WRITING LITERARY ANALYSIS ESSAYS

Choose one of the following literary works and then use prewriting techniques to develop your draft for a literary analysis essay.

Fiction: Short Stories
"Story of an Hour" by Kate Chopin
"The Cathedral" by Raymond Carver
"Everyday Use" by Alice Walker
"The Tell-Tale Heart" by Edgar Allan Poe

Poetry
"Mother to Son" by Langston Hughes
"My Papa's Waltz" by Theodore Roethke
"I heard a Fly buzz—when I died" by Emily Dickinson
"The Road Not Taken" by Robert Frost

Drama
Trifles by Susan Glaspell
A Raisin in the Sun by Lorraine Hansberry
A Doll's House by Henrik Ibsen

⬥ BUILDING SKILLS TOGETHER 11-1: Literary Analysis
▌ Essay Feedback Checklist

Once the rough draft of your literary analysis essay is completed, have a partner read it and answer the following revision and editing questions. You may also use this checklist to revise and edit your own essay.

Revising Essay Structure

☐ Does the introduction capture the attention of the reader? Does it identify the author and title of the work and provide a brief plot summary?

☐ Underline the thesis. Does the thesis statement indicate a clear focus on literary aspects of the work?

☐ Are clear, specific, and related literary elements used as supporting paragraphs? What changes might you make?

☐ Does the writer develop each supporting paragraph using quotations, explanations, summary, and/or paraphrase?

☐ Are the quotations used and punctuated appropriately? What changes might you make?

☐ Does the conclusion end the essay's discussion? What concluding method (restating, observing, remarking, or summarizing) is used? What changes might you make?

☐ Is the point of view in the essay consistent and relevant? Are any changes needed?

☐ How effective is the title in capturing the essay's content? Why or why not?

Editing Spelling, Diction, and Sentence Construction

☐ Are there any misspelled words?

☐ Are appropriate and specific words used?

☐ Are any slang words, text message language, or clichés used?

☐ Consider sentence structure and correct any errors with:

   ☐ Fragments, run-ons, and comma splices

   ☐ Misplaced or dangling modifiers

   ☐ Verb tense consistency

   ☐ Pronoun agreement

   ☐ Subject and verb agreement

Refer to Appendix A for a review of grammar concepts.

Final Assessment

☐ What do you like the most about the essay?

☐ What are you unclear about or have difficulty with in the essay?

UNIT FOUR: Building Essays with Research

F OR SOME ESSAYS like narratives or description, you can use your own ideas to develop your supporting paragraphs; however, in other essays, you may have to supplement your own ideas with research. Research involves looking at material from books, articles, interviews, films, the Internet, and the library. In researching and writing your research essay, the stages of the writing process—prewriting, writing, and rewriting—help you to present your ideas clearly and convincingly. The process of writing a research-based argumentative essay is presented in this unit.

CHAPTER TWELVE: Argumentation
Building Essays with Research

Should you vote for the passage of a new speeding limit? Should smoking on campus be banned? These questions involve taking a position on a debatable issue or one about which people disagree. In courses such as English, political science, and history, you will be asked to take a stand on issues or concerns to persuade others that your position has merit.

Argumentative writing, sometimes called persuasive writing, is powerful because it allows the writer to "put up a fight" in words on meaningful issues. Argumentative writing takes a position on a controversial issue (or problem or concern) and provides reasons and evidence to persuade the reader to agree with the writer. For an issue to be controversial, it must be debatable. If a topic is not controversial, it is difficult to argue for or against it.

 MEMORY TIP

- To **persuade** is to get others to agree with you and to get them to take action.

- To **convince** others is to encourage them to consider the issue, so they understand your position, but they do not have to agree with you or do anything.

For argumentation essays, ideas are supported with research or information from outside sources including books, periodicals, and the Internet. Learning how to write a research-based argumentative paper will sharpen the critical thinking skills you need in most academic classes and careers.

A research paper presents the results of your investigations on a selected topic. Based on your own thoughts and the facts and ideas you have gathered from a variety of sources, a research paper is a creation that is distinctively yours. The experience of gathering, interpreting, and documenting information, developing and organizing ideas and conclusions, and communicating them clearly is an important and satisfying part of your growth as a writer.

> **BUILDING TIP**
>
> Before you learn what writing a researched argumentation essay entails, it is important to understand what a researched essay is <u>not</u>:
>
> - A summary of everything you found on your topic.
> - A repetition of what others have written about the topic.

UNDERSTANDING THE RESEARCH PROCESS

To begin researching for your argumentation essay, you need to follow these two successive steps:

Step 1: Find your topic and position
Step 2: Document the sources to create a bibliography

To see how a research-based argumentation essay takes shape, this chapter will use cloning for a topic as you learn about the steps.

Step 1: Find Your Topic and Position

The first step involves exploring topics to find one that interests you. Often, you are assigned specific topics to research, but sometimes you have to find a topic for your argumentative essay. Your preliminary research is to discover divisive topics, so discuss ideas with your teacher; interview people or librarians; review textbooks, encyclopedia articles, library reference desks, and Internet sites, especially news sites. Look for topics that are controversial; then, narrow your selection to one topic that interests you.

Once you have selected your topic, the next step is to explore or to *do* research about your topic. At this point, you explore the common viewpoints about your topic. The best place to start your exploration is at the college library. Look into print and electronic resources. Your aim is to read the available information about your topic to answer this question: *What opinions are out there about my topic?* Give yourself time to consider the various viewpoints, but be conscious of the deadline for the final draft of your essay. For the cloning example, you would need to determine what advocates and opponents of cloning say.

Throughout your initial exploratory research, you may instinctively lean toward one way of thinking, so write down your preliminary position on the issue, which answers this question: *Are you for or against the issue?* Sometimes you may change your mind on a position depending on what your discoveries reveal, but keep an open mind while you are exploring a topic.

 BUILDING TIP

The easiest way to establish your position is by posing a question about the issue using the word *should.*

Should California adopt the death penalty?

If your answer is yes then you are for the death penalty.

If your answer is no then you are against the death penalty.

Then, using the initial information you gathered about the topic so far, pre-write ideas that answer the *why* question: *Why are you for or against the issue?* As you consider information about your topic, it is good practice to spend time writing out everything you know or have uncovered in your process of exploration. This may help you in two ways: (1) narrow ideas for why you are against or for a controversial topic and (2) determine if there is enough quality information to write a well-supported research paper. During this stage, consider organizing your thoughts by using an outline or a working outline of ideas. A working outline might be an informal list of topics and subtopics you are thinking of covering in your paper. In a working outline, bring related information together under general headings and arrange sections so they relate logically to each other. Use only short phrases to suggest ideas.

 BUILDING TIP

Using an outline can help you organize your ideas and discover connections between pieces of information that you were not aware of when you first thought of your topic. It can also make you aware of material that is not relevant to the purposes of your topic. Refer to Chapter One for a full discussion on formal and informal outlines.

Sometimes an instructor might require that a working outline be submitted at the beginning of your work; your instructor might suggest ways in which the work needs to be further developed or cut back. Your instructor might also see that you are trying to accomplish too much or too little for the scope of the assignment he or she has in mind. The working outline can be revised as you discover new material and new ideas that could be included in your paper.

After you write the research paper, you may want to consider revisiting the working outline to expand it into a final outline or a formal outline that details every idea, support, or evidence you have chosen to include. This practice may help you spot improvement areas in your paper, so you can address them as you rewrite your research paper. If portions of your outline seem weak in comparison to others, more research may be required to create a sense of balance in your argument and presentation. Instructors sometimes require that a final outline be submitted along with the final version of your paper.

Step 2: Document Your Sources

Once you have selected your topic, explored general information about it, determined your position on it, and sketched out a preliminary outline of ideas, you are ready to begin the formal research process of finding, evaluating, and documenting scholarly sources. At this stage, you assess and record information from authoritative reference sources including pertinent books, encyclopedias, or articles in magazines or journals.

Documentation of sources involves two crucial steps in the research process: evaluating sources and taking notes. For many topics, a huge quantity of information may be available, but a low level of quality may be obvious. You do not want to rely on the news in the headlines of tabloids you see near supermarket checkout counters, and it is just as hard to know how much to accept of what is in all the books, magazines, newspapers, journals, Web sites, or various media reports. You need to consider authoritative and reliable sources for your research paper.

Evaluating Sources

Evaluating sources is an important skill. You have to decide where to look, what clues to search for, and what to accept. You may be overwhelmed with too much information or too little. The temptation is to accept whatever you find, but do not be tempted.

 BUILDING TIP

The strength and credibility of your argument will depend directly on the strength and credibility of your sources. One questionable piece of evidence may lead your audience to wonder about the validity of your essay and may affect the extent to which they are persuaded by your argument.

When you use a research or academic library, the books, journals, and other resources have already been evaluated by scholars, publishers, and librarians. Print publishing involves editorial checks that reduce the appearance of inferior information. Every print resource you find has been evaluated in one way or another before you ever read it, which is very different from that of the Internet. For the most part, printed materials are a great source for reliable information. On the

Internet, however, editorial checks exist to a lesser degree. Although criteria for printed materials may be applied to Internet sites, evaluation needs to be more critical in the loose publishing environment of the Internet. When you look at information on the Internet, always evaluate to make sure it is viable information.

> ### ⚒ BUILDING TIP
>
> Many college libraries provide reliable and reputable online databases such as EBSCO Host or ERIC, so you may want to consider using these resources. In addition, resource guides are available for librarians in evaluating, selecting, and organizing published information. They can use this information to direct you in your research.

There is no single, perfect gauge for reliability, truthfulness, or value. Instead, you make an inference from a collection of clues and from what you plan to use from your source. For online sources, look at how credible, accurate, reliable, and timely the sources may be to your position.

- **Credible.** Credibility involves the believability of a source or how much you can trust in what the source presents. For a source to be credible, it needs to be written by a relevant author from a respected publisher. In evaluating the credibility of a source, some questions you might ask may include: Who wrote this information and who is the publisher? Why should I believe this source over another? In determining the credibility of a source, consider:
    - ☐ **Author's credentials.** This includes the author's education, training, and/or experience in the field relevant to the information. Is the author clearly identified? Is there information that is included about the author? Is the author associated with a known organization or company? Is there any way to contact the author for questions or concerns?
    - ☐ **Author's reputation among peers.** Most scholarly journal articles go through a peer review process whereby peer readers examine and approve content before it is published. For print or online articles, look for information about the publisher on organizational Web sites, the words *peer reviewed* or *reviewed* or *edited*, or for shortened forms of information such as abstracts or content summaries. Ask yourself: Was it published from an academic institution for academic purposes? Is it from a news organization written for a wider audience? Has it been produced by an industry, commercial organization, or other resource?

BUILDING TIP

Indicators of lack of credibility include no identification of authorship or anonymity, bad grammar or many misspelled words, and lack of clear quality peer review.

■ **Accurate.** Accuracy involves assuring that the information in the source is actually factually correct, detailed, and comprehensive. An accurate source gives the whole truth about the process of obtaining information. How real is the information? An information source that deliberately leaves out important facts, qualifications, consequences, or alternatives may be misleading or even intentionally deceptive. In evaluating for accuracy, consider the way the information in the source was obtained in the first place. Where did this information come from? What sources did the information creator use? Are the sources listed? Is there a bibliography or other documentation? What kind of support for the information is given? It is especially important for statistics to be documented. Is your source the original researcher or is he or she just reporting someone else's study? Accuracy is often reflected in the tone or style of writing, which can reveal carelessness with detail.

 BUILDING TIP

Indicators of lack of accuracy include no date on the document, vague or sweeping generalizations, and very narrow views of the topic.

■ **Reliable.** Reliability involves examining the source's information for fairness, objectivity, and consistency. To deem a source reliable, consider whether it provides convincing evidence that can be supported by other sources. In effect, how usable is the information? A reliable information source will possess a calm, reasoned tone, arguing or presenting material thoughtfully, without attempting to get you emotionally worked up. Pay attention to the tone and be cautious of highly emotional writing. Consider inquiring whether the source contains valuable research. Does it show new research that is beneficial? Is it trying to persuade the reader to have a certain viewpoint? Can you see any bias in it? Was it written strictly for advertisement purposes or research?

 BUILDING TIP

Indicators of lack of reliability include biased language or tone, exaggerations, sources drawn from authorities known for voicing one position, and lack of valid support and documentation for source information.

■ **Timely.** Timeliness involves how current the work is. Constant advances in disciplines or theories date some work (such as technology news). The facts you learn today may be timely now and outdated tomorrow. Remember to check and recheck your data from time to time, and realize that you will always need to update your facts. Note when the information you find was created, and then decide whether it is still of value to your research. Consider when the material was published. When was the file last updated? Is the information still valid today? Information on the Internet is usually more up-to-date than actual printed publications in books or magazines.

⚒ BUILDING TIP

Indicators of lack of timeliness include today's date on a page other than from a news site. Many Web pages display today's date automatically, regardless of when the content on the page was created.

☞ MEMORY TIP

Consider using the acronym CART to CHECK OUT your research sources.

Credible: How believable is the source?

Who wrote this information and what company published it?

Accurate: How detailed is the source?

How real is the information?

Reliable: How objective is the source?

How usable is the source's information?

Timely: How current is the source?

When was the source published?

Taking Notes

As you evaluate and select reliable and useful sources, take notes on their information, so you have it at the ready to use in your rough draft. As you research, create a list of all the sources you have consulted, even if you may not use them in the essay. This list of works or sources of information that you consulted about your topic is called a **bibliography.** There are various ways to take notes for your bibliography:

■ Using index cards rather than notebook paper may appeal to some because index cards can be shuffled around more easily. Write one idea on each card and include:

  □ Topic of notes in upper-left-hand corner.

☐ Author and title in upper-right-hand corner.

☐ Page numbers on which information was found in lower-right-hand corner.

■ Photocopying or printing sources to highlight or underline important details.

■ Storing notes as computer files because of the ease of transferring material from file to essay draft. Be sure to use a computer storage device as back up to your files.

👆 MEMORY TIP

Copying and pasting information from Web documents or graphics without proper citations or using parts, the entire text, or graphics of someone else's work is **plagiarism** or **cheating,** which may result in a failing grade on the assignment and/or the class.

Whichever note-taking method you choose to use, always remember to record bibliographic information, so you do not plagiarize. Record the source of each piece of information, even if you do not use every piece in your final essay. Generally, for books and magazines, you record the author, title, place of publication, publisher, date of publication, and page numbers. Refer to the "Bibliography and Works Cited" section beginning on page 198 for directions on writing bibliographic entries.

During your research process, as you take notes for your bibliography, it may be helpful to **summarize**, **paraphrase,** or **quote** information from the different sources you consult. In particular, summarizing and paraphrasing provide a quick reference about the information each source provides, so you can judge the relevance of the detail from each source in writing your essay. Moreover, summary and paraphrase are valuable tools in essay writing because they allow you to include other people's ideas without filling up your essay with quotations. However, be sure not to rely heavily on summary and paraphrase because, after all, your ideas are what matter most.

■ **Summary.** You may want to condense a piece of writing to offer it as support for your own ideas. To summarize means to put down the *main ideas* of someone else's work in your own words. This is best used when you want to include many ideas or points from one source. First, absorb the meaning of the source you are looking at; then, capture in your own words the most important ideas from the source.

> ⟨⚒⟩ **BUILDING TIP**
>
> A summary is:
>
> - Shorter than the original since it includes only the main points of the original work and leaves out the irrelevant ideas.
> - About one-third the size of the original piece of writing.
> - Cited with a parenthetical notation at the end to give credit to the original source.

Consider this summary example:

Original Passage

> One reason to fund stem-cell research is that embryos are not humans yet. An embryo, while of value, is not comparable to human life since it is still incapable of existing outside the womb. It may have the potential for life, but it is not a life yet. In his book *Rethinking Life and Death,* Peter Singer contends that embryos are not humans and that life begins when the heartbeat develops, which is during the 5th week of pregnancy, or when the brain begins developing activity, which is detected at 54 days after conception (qtd. in Lee 66). At the time of stem-cell extraction, the embryo cells have not differentiated into organ tissue; therefore, the cell mass is no more human than a slimy mass of organisms. These embryos are not human yet and are to be discarded from the abortion or fertility clinics, so why not use them to help prolong the lives of actual humans?

Summary

> One suggestion for funding stem-cell research is that embryos are not similar to human life because they do not have a beating heart yet and cannot exist outside the womb. Using discarded embryos for stem-cell research is not killing humans (Singer 6).

■ **Paraphrase.** When you paraphrase, you rewrite another writer's words or ideas in your own words without altering the meaning. With paraphrasing, you are not extracting main ideas; rather, you are rephrasing ideas in your own way of writing and language. The paraphrase must be entirely in your own words, so substituting or eliminating phrases here and there is not enough. You need to alter completely the sentence structure, so it is presented in a new form and in your tone of writing. Paraphrasing is a beneficial technique to use in maintaining your own writer's voice in the essay. It can be difficult to find new words for an already well-expressed idea; however, the following strategies may help you.

- ☐ Reread the original passage until you understand its meaning.
- ☐ Set the original aside, and write your paraphrase on a note card.
- ☐ At the top of the note card, write a key word or phrase to indicate the subject of your paraphrase.
- ☐ Check your version with the original to make sure that your version accurately expresses all the essential information in a new form.
- ☐ Use quotation marks to identify any unique term you have borrowed exactly from the source.
- ☐ Record the source (including the page) on your note card so that you can cite it easily if you decide to incorporate the material into your paper.

✂ BUILDING TIP

A paraphrase is:

- The same length as the original since the purpose is to rephrase without leaving out anything, and not to shorten.
- Cited with a parenthetical notation at the end to give credit to the original source.

Consider this paraphrase of the same original passage used for the summary example.

There is controversy around the question of whether embryos used for stem-cell research are considered human life. One source contends that an embryo is not human yet because it does not have a heartbeat, which is the sign of human life. According to Peter Singer, whose book is used to support the source's claim, the 5th week of pregnancy is when embryos develop heartbeats. In addition, the unwanted embryos from abortion or fertility clinics that are used for the removal of stems cells are ones that have not yet reached the 5th week of pregnancy nor are they at the point at which they become human life (Singer 6).

> ### [🖐] MEMORY TIP
>
> Learn how to choose between summarizing and paraphrasing.
>
> Summarize when:
>
> - You want to identify only the main ideas of the writer.
> - You want to simplify and condense a complex idea or ideas.
>
> Paraphrase when:
>
> - You want to use another writer's words without the use of quotes.
> - You want to use another writer's words without plagiarizing.
> - You think that the words of the other writer are too difficult for your readers.

BUILDING SKILLS 12-1: Distinguishing Paraphrase from Summary

Read the following paragraph; then practice your research note-taking skills by summarizing it and then paraphrasing it.

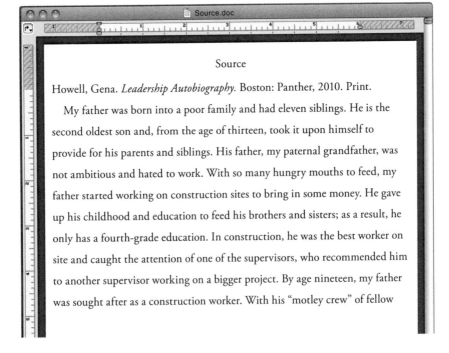

Source

Howell, Gena. *Leadership Autobiography*. Boston: Panther, 2010. Print.

My father was born into a poor family and had eleven siblings. He is the second oldest son and, from the age of thirteen, took it upon himself to provide for his parents and siblings. His father, my paternal grandfather, was not ambitious and hated to work. With so many hungry mouths to feed, my father started working on construction sites to bring in some money. He gave up his childhood and education to feed his brothers and sisters; as a result, he only has a fourth-grade education. In construction, he was the best worker on site and caught the attention of one of the supervisors, who recommended him to another supervisor working on a bigger project. By age nineteen, my father was sought after as a construction worker. With his "motley crew" of fellow workers, he took on a huge construction project in Arizona. In the deserts of Arizona, he built a bigger name for himself and started his own construction company, which became the foundation for his real estate empire.

Page 23

Summary:

_____

_____

Paraphrase:

_____

_____

_____

_____

_____

_____

_____

_____

_____

Bibliography and Works Cited Page

As you consult sources, summarize, paraphrase, and quote information, store your supply of information in a bibliography. A **bibliography** is a list of all outside sources you look up. Keeping a bibliography will ensure that you have the information required to write a Works Cited list. A **Works Cited** list is an alphabetized list of all the sources that you actually use in your essay, and it is the last page of the essay.

> ### ⚒ BUILDING TIP
>
> Your professor may require that you have a bibliography and a Works Cited list for your essay. They both have a specific format that is used; however, there is a difference between those two elements:
>
> - A **bibliography** is a long list of material and sources that you consulted in your research, but did not directly reference in your essay.
> - A **Works Cited** is a shorter list of the sources that you used directly in your essay. It is the last page of your essay with sources arranged alphabetically.

When you refer to a source within your essay, you will use in-text citations or parenthetical notations, which are often the last name of the author(s) and page number(s) in parentheses.

> Hogan (47)

> Furthermore, a large percentage of cloning efforts end in failure; for example, it took "15 pregnancies in 32 surrogate mothers... 276 attempts to clone Dolly the sheep, and nearly 300 eggs had to be fused with cells for the single success story" (Godsen 172).

Your parenthetical notations tie directly to your Works Cited list, which lists the sources from your bibliography that you have referred to or used in the essay.

> Godsen, Roger. *Designing Babies: The Brave New World of Reproductive Technology.* New York: Freeman. 1999. Print.

> **⚒ BUILDING TIP**
>
> Refer to the "Bibliography and Works Cited" section later in the chapter beginning on page 198 for a complete guide on citations.

WRITING AN ARGUMENTATION ESSAY

Once you have gathered all your information as evidence, you should organize the information and determine what patterns or reoccurring ideas emerge from the collected evidence. These ideas help guide your prewriting and provide direction for you to begin writing the essay. Prewrite or list ideas of reasons for or against the issue and narrow them down to the three or so strongest ones. Those three or so reasons make up the supporting paragraphs for your argument. Now, look at your evidence again and decide what you may use to develop your reasons. Have all your evidence available when you get ready to write your essay.

GENERIC PLAN FOR AN ARGUMENTATION ESSAY

Whether you write an outline or a rough draft, here is a brief view of the essential elements in a research paper:

Introduction Paragraph
    Background information on issue
    Thesis = Focused Topic (writer's position about the issue: for or against)

Support Paragraph 1: First reason for or against
    Development Sentences
Support Paragraph 2: Second reason for or against
    Development Sentences
Support Paragraph 3: Most important reason for or against
    Development Sentences
Refutation
    Answer the opposition
Conclusion Paragraph
    Repeat the three reasons
    Call to action

Some writers prefer to write an **outline** first and then the **rough draft,** whereas others prefer writing the rough draft first and then the outline. Refer to Chapter Two for examples on formal and informal outlines.

Using Persuasive Appeals

The goal of argumentative writing is to persuade your audience that your ideas are valid, or more valid than someone else's. To have an effective and persuasive essay, consider connecting with the reader on different levels to impact the perception of your argument. These levels are called **persuasive appeals.** The Greek philosopher Aristotle divided the means of persuasive appeals into three categories— **ethos, pathos, logos.** Persuasive appeals go after the minds, the hearts, and the ethics of people and help influence them to accept ideas and take actions. Throughout your essay, especially in the supporting paragraphs, try to appeal to your reader using a blend of the following appeals:

1. **Logos** is a Greek word for logic. In argumentation, it means using clarity, logical reasons, and supporting evidence to impact the audience. You affect the readers' logic or critical thinking when you use factual information as evidence such as:
    - ☐ Findings from test results
    - ☐ Statistics from surveys
    - ☐ Opinions of experts
    - ☐ Eyewitness testimony
    - ☐ Examples of real cases
2. **Pathos** is a Greek word for emotion. In argumentation, it means persuading by appealing to the reader's emotions. The most common way of conveying a moving appeal is through a story, which can turn the controversial issue into something palpable and present for the reader. Pathos thus refers to both the emotional and the imaginative impact of the message on an audience. The power behind pathos lies in how much the

writer's message moves the audience to make decisions or to take actions. You affect the reader's deeply felt needs and desires when you use stories, powerful images, or shock techniques in relation to such values as:

☐ Achievement: the desire to attain money, fame, acceptance

☐ Independence: the desire to be unique, individual

☐ Conformity: the desire to belong to a group

☐ Endurance: the desire for survival and tolerating burdens

☐ Popularity: the desire to be accepted, respected

☐ Fear: the desire to defeat threats to self, family

3. **Ethos** is a Greek word for ethics. In argumentation, it means convincing the reader through the character of the author. We tend to believe people whom we respect. One of the central problems of argumentation is to project an impression to the reader that you are someone worth listening to, in other words, making yourself, as the author, into an authority on the subject of the paper as well as someone who is likable and worthy of respect. You affect the reader's deeply held core values and ethics when you present strong evidence that affects the readers' perception of:

☐ Religion: the desire to be a good religious follower

☐ Patriotism: the desire to place one's country above all

☐ Humanitarianism: the desire to help others, protect the weak, save the environment

BUILDING SKILLS 12-2: Blending Appeals

Read the following passage and identify the persuasive appeals using the following pattern:

- Underline the sentences with logos.
- Circle the sentences with pathos.
- Bracket the sentences with ethos.

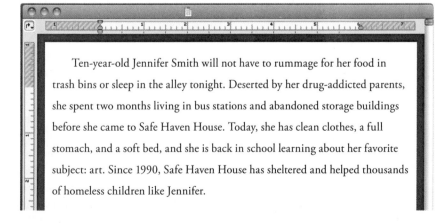

Ten-year-old Jennifer Smith will not have to rummage for her food in trash bins or sleep in the alley tonight. Deserted by her drug-addicted parents, she spent two months living in bus stations and abandoned storage buildings before she came to Safe Haven House. Today, she has clean clothes, a full stomach, and a soft bed, and she is back in school learning about her favorite subject: art. Since 1990, Safe Haven House has sheltered and helped thousands of homeless children like Jennifer.

Safe Haven House's children go on to finish school and get good jobs. In fact, ninety percent of our children finish high school and find steady employment. Safe Haven House has sixty beds under one roof, and, sadly, that is not enough to meet the increasing need. Daily, we have to turn away many of the thousands of homeless children who live in the neighboring streets. Tragically, these children often succumb to prostitution, drugs, abuse, or crime.

Safe Haven House needs your help to build more dorms and expand its job-education center. How can we live in one of the richest cities in the world and ignore the vulnerable children sleeping in our streets? Help us help these forsaken children before they are lost forever.

Contribute to Safe Haven House today.

Introduction Paragraph

In the introduction, you start with an engaging opening that attracts the reader's attention. You may start your introduction with a dramatic question or quotation related to the controversial issue. Then, move into providing historical and social information on your issue, taking into account all the possible positions to help the reader understand the controversy surrounding the issue. In your introduction, provide a clear thesis statement that shows your position on the controversial topic. You may include the thesis statement as your last sentence in the introduction.

As time progresses, our technological breakthroughs advance exponentially. Twenty years ago, there was no way to bring a person's eyesight back to 20/20 without having to wear glasses or contact lenses, but today a ten-minute laser procedure at the ophthalmologist will rid you of most sight impairments. The idea of heart transplant surgery was once considered impossible, whereas today these surgeries have become common. Over time, attitudes toward these advances change and become accepted by society. Continuing medical and technological advances have helped push the limits in science. But the question remains: How far can we push the limits and still create ethical solutions? Just because we can, does it mean we should? Today, the technology and science of genetic engineering has enabled us to create copies of cells and animals. Along the way, it has also allowed for human cloning or the creation of a genetically identical copy of a human being, human cell, or human tissue. Is that acceptable? No, it is morally and ethically wrong to take science and technology so far. Tampering with human creation to artificially reproduce another human is not only murder, but an attempt at playing God.

Thesis Statement

The thesis statement in an argumentation essay includes emphatic language and a clear position on the issue. In one sentence, your thesis statement identifies your position on the issue. The emphatic language you can use includes words such as:

could (not)	need(s)
ought (not)	must have
would (not)	must (not)
It is time	

🖑 MEMORY TIP

Thesis = Focused Topic (position on issue)

Genetic scientists must stop human cloning technology.

BUILDING SKILLS 12-3: Recognizing Argumentation Thesis Statements

Read each sentence and write *TS* next to the ones that are effective argumentation thesis statements and *X* next to those that are not effective argumentation thesis statements.

1. Parents must not spank their children. _____

2. Education is one of the ways to deal with increased drug use among teenagers. _____

3. All Olympic runners are fast. _____

4. An honor student may make a good class president. _____

5. High-sugar foods should not be sold in schools' vending machines. _____

6. Our children would benefit from home schooling. _____

7. Students should not work throughout high school. _____

8. The mayor has proposed building a new toll road to help with the traffic problem. _____

9. Obesity is on the rise in our children, so we need to change the school lunch offerings to healthier ones. _____

10. Global warming is a deepening crisis that we must address and act on wisely and quickly. _____

Supporting Paragraphs

Each supporting paragraph discusses a valid or logical reason for or against the issue to show or prove your position. The reasons should be in order of importance with the last reason as the most important. Consider the following reasons for opposing cloning.

Reason 1: **One reason to stop cloning technology is the inherent health risks and complications associated with the process of cloning.**

Reason 2: **Another reason to stop cloning technology is that it undermines the dignity of human procreation and the conjugal union.**

Reason 3: **The most important reason to stop cloning technology is that it is playing God.**

Development Sentences

Development sentences are sentences you use in the supporting paragraphs to develop each reason. They provide sufficient detail and information to show the importance of each reason to the argument. The developmental sentences in an argumentative essay may present specific ideas taken from your research; therefore, they may include ideas that are summarized, paraphrased, or quoted from your sources. Specifically, they may consist of sentences that show statistics, examples, facts, or expert opinions. To develop your supporting paragraphs, use evidence that shows:

- **Statistics.** Statistics are numbers from surveys or credible research sources.

  Thirteen percent of death-row inmates are executed every year.

- **Examples of cases.** Examples of cases are specific experiences or stories that have happened.

  1973's *Roe vs. Wade* case on the issue of abortion.

- **Facts.** Facts are statements that can be verified or proven in some way.

  Martin Luther King, Jr., was killed on April 4, 1968, in Memphis, Tennessee.

- **Expert opinions.** Expert opinions are the opinions of credentialed people who are expert in their fields such as forensic pathologists, court judges, FBI agents, or doctors' or psychologists' diagnoses or prognoses.

According to Henry Lee, famous forensic scientist, the evidence in the case leads to the conclusion that the crime was committed 72 hours before the criminal called law enforcement.

 MEMORY TIP

An easier way to remember evidence in persuasive writing is to use the acronym SEFEs.

Statistics

Examples

Facts

Expert Opinions

Remember this statement: In an argument, to be safe, use SEFEs.

Much of your evidence (or SEFEs) may be quoted material. Quotations help you make an impact on your reader because they increase the power of your arguments and make your essay more interesting and believable. Use quotations when the words from the source would be memorable or authoritative, or when paraphrasing or summarizing would change the meaning of the original text's words or phrases. However, do not string quotes together as developmental sentences because they may distract the reader and affect your writer's voice. Consider using them when they can make a strong impact in supporting important ideas. The most common information you cite in your essay is a direct quotation. Use direct quotes when you draw on a person's exact words from an interview, book, article, or document. This technique requires the use of quotation marks (" ") and the recording of the words or phrases exactly as they appear in the original document. Follow or precede your quotes with sentences that explain the relevance of the quote to your reason. At the end of each quotation, throughout your essay, give the parenthetical note.

 BUILDING TIP

Refer to Appendix C: Quotations Protocol for a full explanation on the use of quotations.

Refutation Paragraph

After you state and develop your reasons in the body paragraphs, you need to refute (prove false, rebut, counter) the opposing side to defend and protect your argument. Refutations make the writer look credible as they show the reader that you come to your position on the issue fully knowledgeable of all the valid arguments on the issue. You have weighed all sides before drawing conclusions.

Refutations also strengthen the writer's argument by weakening the opposing side's argument. Refutation allows the writer to acknowledge, politely and without ridicule, the other sides' opinion and address its main or most important objection to your position head-on. That way, the writer counters the objection and shows the weakness in the opposition. Consider this example using the cloning topic.

Many are of the view that cloning saves lives by providing "spare parts" to people with devastating conditions and diseases. Advocates of this human therapeutic cloning believe the practice could provide genetically identical cells for regenerative medicine and tissues and organs for transplantation. *— Main objection*

But have they ever wondered that in creating that clone for spare parts, we are actually creating then killing a human person with a soul and a brain? In other words, to get "parts" for a human, they must kill one. *— Refutation to main objection*

This is morally wrong! William Keeler maintains "creating human life solely to cannibalize and destroy it is the most unconscionable use of human cloning" (Keeler 47). What about using science and technology to use animal parts or to create artificial "spare parts"? That does not involve human killing. Consider the cases where animal organs where used; the most recent animal-to-human transplant involved 15-day-old Baby Fae, a California girl who received a heart from a baboon in 1984 (Keeler 47). *— Support for refutation*

TRANSITIONS USED IN ARGUMENTATION ESSAYS

also	above all	in fact
another fact to consider	especially	worst of all
another reason	most important (ly)	

See Appendix B for a full list of transitions.

Conclusion Paragraph

The objective of the conclusion is to end the discussion; therefore, you may restate, in the order they were presented, the main reasons for your position and reword the thesis sentence. You may also end with a strong call to action or a final observation. A call to action is an invitation to the reader to get up and do what you suggest in order to bring about change.

BUILDING TIP

A call to action is a sentence(s) that urges the readers to do, change, adopt, or stop something.

I urge you to march for freedom.
Join us in stopping cloning.

Remember to keep your conclusion short and to close off your discussion. Consider this example of what a conclusion paragraph could look like for cloning.

> Although cloning technology offers hope to those fighting debilitating conditions, those wanting to replace the deceased, and infertile couples wanting offspring, *— Restatement of reasons*
>
> it is wrong to condone a process riddled with complications and risks, to undermine the process of procreation and conjugal union, and most importantly to play God. *— Position on the topic*
>
> The expectations of great wonders from cloning only lead to corruption and risk, so I urge you to stop this atrocity. *— Call to action*

Title

The title in an argumentative essay has to reflect the overall discussion of the essay. It may be in two parts: the first part is the issue and the second part is the writer's position on it. Or, it may be in one part that is creative and reflective of your discussion.

Two-part titles:

Cloning: The Key to Immortality

One-part titles:

Cloning and Immorality

Bibliography and Works Cited

Documenting sources helps you tell your readers where you found the information (quotation, paraphrase, or summary) you used in your essay, so that if they choose to, your readers can find the information themselves. As you cite or document your sources in the bibliography and in the Works Cited page, you may need to follow different citation guidelines such as APA (American Psychological Association) or MLA (Modern Language Association). Generally, for an English course, you will be required to use the MLA style in your essays. The MLA style calls for inserting in-text citations or **parenthetical notations** in your essay after quotations, summaries, or paraphrases and the creation of a **Works Cited page** at the end of your paper that shows the corresponding sources for each parenthetical notation.

 MEMORY TIP

MLA requirements may change, so be sure to reference the most recent MLA guidelines by visiting www.mla.org.

Rules for In-Text Citations or Parenthetical Notations

When you use a quotation, paraphrase, or summary from outside sources, use parenthetical notation in the body of the paper. A parenthetical notation appears at the end of the quotations, summary, or paraphrase, and it is placed in parentheses (hence its name). That notation refers to and corresponds with an entry in a works-cited list at the end of the essay. A typical parenthetical reference includes:

- The author's last name and page number in parentheses.

  Everyone laughed when she said, "Life is good" (Hogan 47).

- The page number only in parentheses if the author's name is clearly identified in the text.

  According to Gina Hogan, "Life is good" (47).

Rules for the Works Cited List

The Works Cited list includes all the works you referred to or cited in your essay. Use the following guidelines to help you prepare your list:

1. Begin your Works Cited list on a new page at the end of your essay.
2. Number the Works Cited page as the next page of your essay.
3. Center the heading *Works Cited* one inch from the top of the page and begin typing each entry at the left-hand margin.
4. Double-space the list.
5. List entries alphabetically according to author's last name.
6. Indent second and subsequent lines one-half inch.

The following entries show the most common Works Cited entries and parenthetical references you may encounter.

Books

Last name of author, First name of author. *Full Title.* Place of Publication: Publisher, Publication date. Medium of Publication.

One Author:

> Hogan, Gina. Building Better Grammar. Boston: Cengage Learning, 2013. Print.
>
> Parenthetical notation: (Hogan 12)

Two Authors:

> Kirkley, Shannon, and Gloria McCann. You Can Clean Anything. New York: Sutton, 1999. Print.
>
> Parenthetical notation: (Kirkley, McCann 23-26)

More Than Three Authors:

> James, Raoul, et al. The American Promise. Boston: Bedford/St. Martin's, 2003. Print.
>
> Parenthetical notation: (Raoul et al. 98)

Periodicals

Magazine Article:

Last name of author, First name of author. "Article Title." *Name of Magazine* Day Month Year: pages. Medium of publication.

> Jackson, Jerry. "A Tragic Mistake." Newsweek 3 Mar. 2006: 41-45. Print.
>
> Parenthetical notation: (Jackson 41-45)

Newspaper Article:

Last name of author, First name of author. "Article Title." *Name of Periodical* Day Month Year: pages. Medium of publication.

> Adler, Michelle. "Making Sense of Cloning." Boston Globe 28 Mar. 2008: 98. Print.
>
> Parenthetical notation: (Adler)

Internet Sources

When citing Internet sources, include any information you can find such as the name of the author, title of the work, title of site, publisher or sponsor, the date of publication, date of access. Include the word *Web* for the medium of publication. It is not necessary to include the Web address or URL since readers can usually find the source by typing the author's name or title. Sometimes, you could include the URL if your instructor requires it or if you think readers might need it to locate the source. In that case, enclose the URL in angle brackets like so: <www.buildingwriting.com>.

A Web Site:
Editor, author, or compiler name (if available). *Name of Site*. Title of Website. Sponsor site, Publication date. Medium of publication. Date of access.

> The Purdue Owl Family of Sites. The Writing Lab and OWL at Purdue.
> Purdue U, 2009. Web. 23 Apr. 2009.
>
> Parenthetical notation: (Purdue Owl)

An Article in a Web Magazine:
Author name. "Article Title." *Title of Web Magazine*. Publisher name, Publication date. Medium of publication. Date of access.
Use *n.p.* if no publisher name is available and *n.d.* if no publishing date is given.

> Burns, Mark. "The Youth Industry." Atlantic Online. Atlantic Monthly
> Group, Dec. 2002. Web. 3 Jan. 2009.
>
> Parenthetical notation: (Burns)

Article in an Online Reference Book or Encyclopedia:
"Title." *Title of Online Reference Book/Encyclopedia*. Publisher name, Publication date. Medium of publication. Date of access.

> "Lebanon." Infoplease World Atlas and Map Library. Pearson
> Education, 2010. Web. 29 Jan. 2010.
>
> Parenthetical notation: ("Lebanon")

Article in an Online Scholarly Journal:
Author(s) name. "Article Title." *Title of Scholarly Journal* Volume. Issue (Year): pages. Medium of publication. Date of access.

Dalley, Nadine. "Emerging Issues in Youth Culture and Policy: Current Conditions and Future Directions." Social Work and Society: The International Online-Only Journal 6.2 (2008): 541-543. Web. 20 May 2009.

Parenthetical notation: (Dalley)

Personal Web Site:
Author(s) name. Title of Online Page. Sponsor of page. Publication date or last update. Medium of publication. Date of access.

Thompson, Doug. Home page. Doug Thompson, 5 Feb 2010. Web 10 July 2010. <http://www.Thompson.com.

Parenthetical notation: (Thompson)

Editorial:
Author name. "Article Title." Editorial. *Title of Publication*. Publisher name, Publication date. Medium of publication. Date of access.

"Teacher Layoffs in the LAUSD." Editorial. Los Angeles Times. Los Angeles Times, 4 Jan. 2010. Web. 12 July 2010.

Parenthetical notation: ("Teacher Layoffs in the LAUSD")

Other Sources
Personal Interview:

Sawyer, Don. Personal interview. 12 June 2007.

Film:

Casino. Dir. Martin Scorsese. Perf. Robert De Niro, Joe Pesci, James Woods, Sharon Stone, and Kevin Pollak. Universal, 1995. Film.

NOTE: For parenthetical notations of some sources, like personal interview and film, mention the source in the text. For example:

Interviewed in 2007, Kelly stated that critics failed to see the real theme in her novel.

Heists and corruption is the underlying focus of Scorsese's Casino.

BUILDING SKILLS 12-4: Citing Sources

Out of class, search for and cite source material. Follow these directions:

1. Find three to five recent works on a topic that interests you or one that is likely to appear in both print and electronic sources. If you do not have a topic of interest, you may consider one of the following: *medical marijuana, assisted suicide, designer babies,* or *genetically engineered foods.*

2. Your three to five sources should be of different kinds, such as a book, a journal or magazine article, a film/video, a Web article, and a Web site. Your research must include different kinds of sources.

3. Evaluate each source, take notes using quotations, summary, or paraphrasing; then, record bibliographic information for works cited entries.

4. Using the MLA style for citations, create a works cited page for your sources.

EXAMPLE OF AN ARGUMENTATION ESSAY

Lebeau 1

Phil Lebeau
Professor Hogan
ENG 100
Oct. 23, 2012

Cloning: The Corruption of Mankind

As time progresses, the technological breakthroughs advance exponentially. Twenty years ago there was no way to bring a person's eyesight back to 20/20 without having to wear glasses or contact lenses, but today a ten-minute laser procedure at the ophthalmologist will eliminate most sight impairments. The idea of heart transplant surgery was once considered impossible whereas today these surgeries have become common. Over time, attitudes toward these advances change and become accepted by society. Continuing medical and technological advances have helped push the limits in science. But the question remains: How far can the limits be pushed and still create ethical solutions? Just because we can, does it mean we should? Today, the technology and science of genetic engineering has enabled us to create copies of cells and animals. Along the way, it has also allowed for human cloning or the creation of a genetically identical copy of a human being, human cell, or human tissue. Is that acceptable? No, it is morally and ethically wrong to take science and technology so far. Tampering with human creation to artificially reproduce another human is not only murder, but an attempt at playing God. The German philosopher Immanuel Kant said it best: "Man, however, is not a thing, and thus not something to be used merely as means; he must always be regarded in all his actions as an end in himself. Therefore, I cannot dispose of man in my own person as to mutilate, corrupt, or kill him . . ." (Kant 312). We must stop the technology of human cloning.

Lebeau 2

One reason to stop human cloning technology is the health risks and complications associated with the process of cloning. Many attempts at animal cloning created disfigured monsters with severe abnormalities: "A recent study of mammalian cloning suggests that a number of defects often created in the reprogramming of the egg do not manifest themselves until later in the life of the resulting clone, so that the mature clones have often undergone spectacular, unforeseen deaths" (McGee). The disfigured embryos are mostly destroyed in the womb, but some of these abnormalities do not appear until after birth and necessitate their killing at a point when the animal or baby has matured. In fact, Dolly, the first sheep to be cloned from an adult somatic cell, suffered from arthritis at an early age and at the age of six died prematurely of severe lung disease. Furthermore, a large percentage of cloning efforts end in failure; for example, it took "15 pregnancies in 32 surrogate mothers... 276 attempts to clone Dolly the sheep, and nearly 300 eggs had to be fused with cells for the single success story" (Godsen 172). Since sheep have a fertility rate 3 to 4 times greater than that of humans, it would take hundreds of surrogate mothers to produce one successfully cloned infant. That would mean that there would be a great amount of miscarriages, still births, and infants born with potentially serious and unpredictable birth defects. In fact, Dixon contends that "if the adult the genetic material was gathered from was someone thirty years old, there is a possibility that the child born would also be thirty years old at birth, therefore shortening his/her life span and shattering the hopes of the parents" (Dixon 32). How many discarded embryos and sick, aged, or disfigured infants would we need to go through to have one successfully cloned human? Is human life so dispensable? Humans are not commodities to be treated as things. And if it should get to that point where humans are "things" then who will ensure quality control? What is to stop scientists from taking this technology too far and creating humanoid monsters such as

Mary Shelley's *Frankenstein*? The temptation would be there to shape the human gene pool and breed desired strains of human life. We would have living human monsters, and just imagine if this technology got into the wrong hands, like the historical dictators that have risen to power to oppress others; we would be fighting a losing battle against ourselves.

In addition, cloning technology undermines the dignity of human procreation and the marital union. Human procreation involves a man and a woman coming together as one. A child is not something owed to one, but a gift. The supreme gift of marriage is a human person. A child may not be considered a piece of property but a human who possesses genuine rights: the right to be the fruit of the specific act of the conjugal love of his parents, and the right to be respected as a person from the moment of his conception. Reproductive technology erases the human factor in the procreation process and turns it into an artificial and technological process. In a sense, cloning is a way to make babies without sexual intercourse and emotion. Furthermore, a child is a living expression of mutual love between two individuals, and it is far more practical to have a child within the environment of marriage and family than in a laboratory.

Some are of the view that cloning would help infertile couples produce an offspring (Brock 146). However, while cloning could provide a longed-for offspring, it brings with it emotional risks. A cloned child would have to deal with the confusion of who her parents are because as she grows up knowing that her mother is her sister, her father is her brother-in-law, and her brother is her nephew, the process of self-identity for both the clone and the parents is worsened by emotional confusion. What happens to a family when the father sees his wife's clone grow up into the copy of the twenty-year-old he fell in love with and married years ago? Should a sexual relationship ensue, it would "be with the wife's twin, no incest is involved technically" (Dixon). Through the clone, the mother sees herself growing up all over again. In the

Lebeau 4

case of the clone being a replacement for a deceased child, the grieving process is suspended because the sense of loss is eliminated by the presence of the cloned replacement. Psychiatrists agree that this fabricated family environment where a loved one is brought back from the dead wreaks havoc on the family unit's emotional well-being. The great expectation that the cloned replacement is the same as the lost family member places significant mental, emotional, and social pressure on the replacement. In essence, the cloned child would live in the shadow of its donor and that impedes its psychological and social development. As George Smith claims, "Although programmed conception may well be more humane than chance, the most serious argument advanced thus far against human cloning is that it disrupts a more authentic form of self-discovery, or in other words, it compromises personal liberty in the name of advancing science" (262). In the end, there is a greater purpose for those who cannot bear children and those who die early.

The most important reason to stop cloning technology is that it is playing God. Playing God refers to someone taking on the role of God in making human-related decisions; for example, deciding who is to live or die. Humans evolve from the natural union of man and woman and through God's will and intent. When we select genes and implant them into an embryo, we are "engineering" our own children and taking God out of the picture. Then, who decides who gets a clone? Will wealth be the deciding factor? Who is to stop scientists from cloning the elites like Albert Einstein or Bill Gates? Who decides the appropriate purposes for cloning? Will the clones be seen as God's children allowed into heaven? Cloning allows man to usurp God as the almighty creator and designer of life. In that way, man can create genetically perfect humans by cloning whoever fits a purpose. For example, infertile couples can go in to get "designer babies" where they pick their personal preference in what they want their child to look like. Godsen claims, "the fear of choosing other personal preferences beyond eye color, such as

Lebeau 5

high IQ or a certain aptitude . . .is not a consideration" (110–111). In effect, a child will no longer be considered a blessing from God, but rather a product manufactured by a scientist, and man is created being of man instead of by God. If humans are able to select their own children, the diversity in the world would diminish, and we will slip into the dangerous area of making a master people or a master race. This creates a new type of discrimination where humans are stripped of their individuality. Narcissists could abuse this technology by cloning themselves and giving others the hope of immortality through the act of playing God.

Many are of the view that cloning saves lives by providing "spare parts" to people with devastating conditions and diseases. Advocates of this "human healing" cloning believe the practice could provide genetically identical cells for recreation and tissues and organs for transplantation. But, have they ever wondered that in creating that clone for spare parts we are actually creating and then killing a human person with a soul and a brain? In other words, to get "parts" for a human, they must kill one. This is morally wrong! William Keeler maintains "creating human life solely to cannibalize and destroy it is the most unconscionable use of human cloning" (47). What about using science and technology to use animal parts or to create artificial "spare parts?" That does not involve human killing. Consider the cases where animal organs were used; the most recent animal-to-human transplant involved 15-day-old Baby Fae, a California girl who received a heart from a baboon in 1984 (Keeler 47). Then consider the artificial organs and limbs that have been produced: The first case came in 1982, when the Jarvik-7 artificial heart was transplanted in the chest of Barney Clark of Salt Lake City, Utah (Keeler 47). Artificial lungs made their first appearance in animal tests in 1996, the same year that "six biotech companies put artificial blood products on the market" (Godsen 111). The advances are even more apparent with knee replacements. Most physicians are advocating the use of artificial organs and limbs because

Lebeau 6

they do not want to "play God" by murdering humans for spare parts. They, like Soren Holm, feel "there is some core of truth in the assertion that it is deliberately wrong to try to create a copy of an already existing human being" (36).

Although cloning technology offers hope to those fighting debilitating conditions, those wanting to replace the deceased, and infertile couples wanting offspring, it is wrong to condone a process riddled with complications and risks, to undermine the process of procreation and conjugal union, and most importantly, to play God. Cloning is not a reliable medical technology source that would benefit mankind because, as Godsen contends, "if we ever try cloning humans, we must remember that it will never be playacting, for if we make a mistake then a whole life could be killed" (142). The expectations of great wonders from cloning only lead to corruption and risk, so I urge you to stop this atrocity.

Works Cited

Brock, Dan W. "Cloning Human Beings: An Assessment of the Ethical Issues: Pro and Con." Clone and Clones. Eds. Martha C. Nussbaum and Cass R. Sunstein. New York: Norton, 1998. Print.

Chitty, Mary. "A Clone of Your Own? The Science and Ethics of Cloning." Library Journal 130.17 (2005): 77. Health Source: Nursing/Academic Edition. Web. 21 Jan. 2008.

Devolder, K. "What's in a Name? Embryos, Entities, and Antities in the Stem Cell Debate." Journal of Medical Ethics 32.1 (2006): 43–8. Web. 6 Apr. 2008.

Dixon, Patrick. "Reasons Against Cloning." Global Change 11 Nov. 2003. Print.

Dudley, W., ed. The Ethics of Human Cloning. San Diego: Green Haven P, 2001. Print.

Godsen, Roger. Designing Babies: The Brave New World of Reproductive Technology. New York: Freeman, 1999. Print.

Holm, Soren. "Cloning Could Place an Unfair Burden on Clones." The Ethics of Human Cloning. Ed. William Dudley. San Diego: Green Haven P, 2002. Print.

Kant, Immanuel. "Foundations of the Metaphysics of Morals." Exploring Philosophy: An Introductory Anthology. New York: Oxford UP, 2000. Print.

Keeler, William. "Cloning Human Embryos for Medical Purposes Is Unethical." The Ethics of Human Cloning. Ed. William Dudley. San Diego: Green Haven P. Print.

McGee, Glenn. "Primer on Ethics and Human Cloning." Action Bio Science Mag. 18 Nov. 2007. Web. 4 Oct. 2008.

Smith II, George P. Bioethics and the Law: Medical, Socio-legal and Philosophical Directions for a Brave New World. Lanham: UP of America, 1998. Print.

● BUILDING SKILLS TOGETHER 12-1: Evaluating
■ Argumentation Essays

Working in a small group, read each of the following essays and answer the evaluation questions that follow. Note: These essays have in-text citations.

Don't Stem-Cell Research

Embryonic stem-cell research is the latest controversy to be discussed in the press. What is the controversy all about? Embryonic stem cells are the cells found in unborn human embryos. Human life begins as a fertilized egg after the union of an ovum and sperm; then, it divides and differentiates into many cells called blastocyst, which contain about 100 cells that are stem cells (Lee 61). These stem cells can be kept alive indefinitely if grown in cultures and can grow into almost any kind of cell. To extract them, the embryo must be killed at the cell stage, not having formed human features yet. Stem-cell research then is research involving the creation, usage, and destruction of embryonic stem cells in humans. Opponents of this kind of research claim that it requires that a human life be killed. Proponents of this kind of research claim that researching and using embryonic stem cells may hold the answer to many medical advances in the near future. That the embryos used for research are aborted embryos or donated excess embryos created for in-vitro fertilization, which are to be destroyed, or stored for a long time, past their viable storage life. We must keep and fund stem-cell research.

First off, the source of the embryos used in research are aborted fetuses from abortion clinics or excess embryos frozen in nitrogen from fertility clinics to be destroyed, or stored for long periods of time, past their viable storage life (David 369). These embryos are going to be destroyed or trashed anyway, so why not use them for valuable research? It would be a more efficient and practical use for the discarded embryos. In 2004, in a presidential debate, John Kerry discussed ethically guided embryonic stem-cell research. He claimed we have "100,000 to 200,000 embryos frozen in nitrogen today from fertility clinics. These were not taken from abortion or something like that. They were from a fertility clinic, and they are either going to be destroyed or left frozen. And I believe if we have the option, which scientists tell us we do, of curing Parkinson's, curing diabetes, curing, you know, some kind of a . . . you know, paraplegic or quadriplegic or, you know, a spinal cord injury — anything that's the nature of the human spirit. I think it is respecting life to reach for that cure" (qtd. in Turner 4).

The second reason to fund stem-cell research is that embryos are not humans yet. An embryo, while of value, is not comparable to human life while it is still incapable of existing outside the womb. It may have the potential for life, but it is not a life yet. In his book *Rethinking Life and Death*, Peter Singer contends that embryos are not humans and that life begins when the heartbeat develops, which is during the 5th week of pregnancy, or when the brain begins developing activity, which is detected at 54 days after conception (qtd. in Lee 66). At the time of stem-cell extraction, the embryo's cells have not differentiated into organ tissue; therefore, the cell mass is no more human than a slimy mass of organisms. These embryos are not human yet and are to be discarded from the abortion or fertility clinics, so why not use them to help prolong the lives of actual humans? The psychiatrist Elisabeth KüBler-Ross says, "We have to ask ourselves whether medicine is to remain a humanitarian and respected profession or a new but depersonalized science in the service of prolonging life rather than diminishing human suffering" (David 379).

Stem cells offer several cures for diseases, many of which are life-threatening. Embryonic stem cells are nondesignated cells; they can be placed where they are needed. As a result, they can be manipulated to regrow and redifferentiate into healthier cells. In recent studies, stem cells have been shown to cure mild cases of diabetes and certain kinds of cancers. According to Steinbock, doctors in Berlin reported curing a man of AIDS by giving him transplanted blood stem cells from an embryo (29). Scientists have hopes for cures for Parkinson's disease, Autoimmune Disease, Cerebral Palsy, Heart Failure, Cancer, and Rheumatoid Arthritis.

Opponents of embryonic stem-cell research argue in favor of less risky cell alternatives, such as those involving adult stem cells, which are extracted from the bone marrow or involving cord cells, which are extracted from the umbilical cord blood. However, according to Hines's report, adult stem cells exist as minor residents within a mature adult; only 1 cell out of every 1,000 cells of the bone marrow could be a useable stem cell as opposed to the usefulness of most of the embryonic stem-cell population. Additionally, adult stem cells do not divide fast enough to offer immediate treatment, lack plasticity, and are harder to manipulate and to regrow.

We should fund embryonic stem-cell research because it makes good use of aborted and frozen or discarded fetuses, it does not involve the killing of a human since embryos are not humans yet, and it affords us the ability to cure diseases. If your son or daughter is battling cancer, you would go to whatever lengths to help and to cure him or her. Stem-cell research is the end that justifies the means. With all the potential for it, I ask you to join me in furthering funding for stem-cell research.

Works Cited

David, Matthew, and Jamieson Kirkhope. "Cloning/Stem Cells and the Meaning of Life." *Current Sociology* 53.2 (2005): 367–81. Print.

Hines, Paul J., Barbara A. Purnell, and James Marx. "Stem Cells Branch Out. Introduction: Special Section on Stem Cell Research and Ethics." *Science* 287.5457 (2000). Web. 25 Feb. 2008.

Lee, Patrick, and Roland P. George. "The First Fourteen Days of Human Life." *New Atlantis* 13 (2006): 61–7. Print.

Steinbock, Bart. "The Morality of Killing Human Embryos." *The Journal of Law, Medicine & Ethics : A Journal of the American Society of Law, Medicine & Ethics* 34.1 (2006): 26–34. Print.

Turner, Lin. "The Media and the Ethics of Cloning." *The Chronicle of Higher Education* 44.5 (1997): 4–5. Print.

Punishment by Death

The death penalty is the legal infliction of death as a penalty for killing a person. Throughout history, various forms of wrongdoing have been punishable by death. Methods of execution have included practices such as crucifixion, drowning, stoning, burning at the stake, hanging, impaling, and beheading. Today, the death penalty is accomplished by lethal gas or injection, electrocution, hanging, or shooting. Most industrialized nations have put a stop to the death penalty and substituted it with long terms of imprisonment until death. The U.S. federal government and most of its states allow the death penalty. It is time to abolish the death penalty in our American justice system.

First of all, the death penalty is not a crime deterrent. Our overflowing prisons point to the fact that the threat of punishment by death has not deterred criminals from committing crimes. In fact, the number of prisoners on death row has grown nationally by an average of 5% every year since 2001 (Bedau 21). Furthermore, the murderer is not of sound mind and judgment while committing the crime. Since the killer does not think about the consequences of his crime, the threat of death is not a forethought. According to the *Journal of the Institute for the Advancement of Criminal Justice (IACJ)*, crime studies done in Maryland show that most murders are crimes of passion committed under the blinding influences of hatred, rage, jealousy, or fear with no thought to repercussions. It is clear that the threat of death does not stop a person from murdering.

The second reason is the cost of the death penalty. Because it involves so many required post-trial hearings, reviews, and appeals, the death penalty costs more than life imprisonment. According to *IACJ*'s 2008 records of the State Comptroller of Los Angeles, the average cost of a trial in a federal death case is $620,932, about 8 times that of a murder case in which the death penalty is not sought. If California alone replaced the death penalty with a sentence of life without parole, the state would save more than $130 million each year on court proceedings. Those same *IACJ* records show the average cost of actually executing *a prisoner* in California is a flabbergasting $25 million while the estimated total cost of life without parole per prisoner is a reasonable $1.2 million. A new study by the Urban Institute in March 2008 found that Maryland taxpayers have paid $37.2 million for each of the state's five executions since 1978, the year that state reinstated the death penalty (Bedau 39). The study estimates the average cost to Maryland taxpayers for each death sentence is $3 million, which is about $2 million more than the cost of a case with no death penalty (Bedau 42).

The most important reason is human rights. All humans have an inherent right to dignity and life. Every person's life is worthy of regard, and life in prison respects a human's life while the death penalty devalues it as if it is a bone to be tossed aside. It is more humane to let a person live on life without parole than to kill him or her. After all, by killing him or her, are we not committing the very same crime that person committed against another? Furthermore, studies have shown that a person sentenced to the death penalty experiences most of the torment in the time leading to the execution (Bedau 56). According to criminologist Robert Johnson, 70% of death-row inmates suffer from severe depression and symptoms of psychosis in the months prior to the execution (qtd. in Godfrey 89). Furthermore, death-row inmates are not allowed to socialize with other inmates. They spend twenty-three hours a day in a small cell. The isolation coupled with extreme anxiety and fear of death can be extremely destructive to the inmates' mental and emotional states.

Some argue that since the murderer has taken the life of another, he or she should be punished by having her/his life taken for justice to be served. But what about the mistakes that have been made where the sentenced person turns out not to be the one who committed the crime? Consider the case of Kirk Bloodsworth of Maryland. According to the *Journal of the Institute for the Advancement of Criminal Justice*, in 1985, Bloodsworth was sentenced to death for rape and murder and in 1993, before his execution, newly available DNA evidence proved that he was not the rapist-killer, and he was released. Our justice system is not perfect and mistakes can be made. The death penalty is irreversible, and people have been wrongfully executed. Anything that involves even one error like this is unacceptable.

The death penalty does not deter crime, save money, or treat criminals humanely. Until our justice system is infallible and error is exterminated, we have no right to take the life of another human being. As Helen Prejean says, in *Dead Man Walking,* "Our Government . . . can't be trusted to control its own bureaucrats or collect taxes equitably or fill a pothole, much less decide which of its citizens to kill." For our collective safety, abolish the death penalty.

Works Cited

Bedau, Hugo A. *The Death Penalty in America.* New York: Oxford UP, 1982. Print.

Godfrey, Michael J., and Vincent Schiraldi. *How Have Homicide Rates Been Affected by California's Death Penalty?* San Francisco: Center on Juvenile and Criminal Justice, 1995. Print.

The Journal of the Institute for the Advancement of Criminal Justice: Issue #2: The Death Penalty in California. Sacramento: IACJ, 2007. May 2007. Web. 18 July 2008.

The Journal of the Institute for the Advancement of Criminal Justice: Issue #5: The Death Penalty in Maryland. Annapolis: IACJ, 2008. Apr. 2008. Web. 24 June 2008.

1. Consider the introduction. Does the writer offer background information on the issue? What method is used to "hook" the reader's interest? Does the introduction offer sufficient background information sentences about the topic?

_____

_____

_____

2. Underline the thesis statement. Is the thesis statement clearly stated and contains strong persuasive language? Is the thesis statement effective? What might you change or add?

_____

_____

_____

3. How many supporting paragraphs are used to develop the thesis? Are they sufficient to supporting the argument?

_____

_____

_____

4. Is each supporting paragraph supported by strong evidence (or SEFEs: Statistics, Examples, Fact, Expert Opinions)? How so? What might you change or add?

_____

_____

_____

5. Where does the author use logos, pathos, and ethos? List a few. Do you think the appeals used are sufficient or does the writer need to offer more?

_____

_____

_____

6. Circle the transition words or expressions. Are they effective in moving you through the supporting paragraphs? List them and determine the order they show.

_____

_____

_____

7. What does the writer offer as a rebuttal or refutation to the opposing side? How strong is that refutation?

_____

_____

_____

8. Is there a conclusion paragraph? How does it end the essay's discussion? What method(s) (restating, observing, remarking, or summarizing) is used to conclude? Does it leave the reader with a call to action? Explain your answer.

_____

_____

_____

9. What point of view is being used in this essay? Is it effective for the argument? Explain your answer.

_____

_____

_____

10. Is the title effective? Why or why not?

_____

_____

_____

SUGGESTED TOPICS FOR WRITING ARGUMENTATION ESSAYS

Choose one of the following topics or use one of your own and then use prewriting techniques to develop your draft for an argumentation essay.

| Censorship of books or rap music |
| The use of grades for performance in education |
| Home schooling |
| Paternity leave from work |
| Dating services |
| The Green Movement |
| Obesity in America |
| Whistle-blowing |
| Glass ceiling |
| Bilingualism in American schools |

▮ BUILDING SKILLS TOGETHER 12-2: Argumentation Essay Feedback Checklist

Once the rough draft of your research essay is completed, have a partner read it and answer the following revision and editing questions. You may also use this checklist to revise and edit your own essay.

Revising Essay Structure

☐ Does the introduction capture the attention of the reader? Are there sufficient introductory sentences before the thesis statement? What changes might you make?

☐ Underline the thesis. Does it include a clear position on the topic? What changes might you make?

☐ Are clear, specific, and related reasons used as supporting paragraphs? What changes might you make?

☐ Is each supporting paragraph sufficiently developed with enough evidence (or SEFEs)? Where can you make improvements?

☐ Are there clear transition words to move you through the body paragraphs? Where might you make changes?

☐ Does the writer offer a rebuttal or refutation to the opposing side? How strong is that refutation?

☐ Does the conclusion summarize the supporting ideas, restate the thesis statement, and offer a strong call to action? What changes might you make?

☐ Is the point of view in the essay consistent and relevant? Are any changes needed?

☐ How effective is the title in capturing the essay's content? Why or why not?

Editing Spelling, Diction, and Sentence Construction

☐ Are there any misspelled words?

☐ Are appropriate and specific words used?

☐ Are any slang words, text message language, or clichés used?

☐ Consider sentence structure and correct any errors with:

    ☐ Fragments, run-ons, and comma splices

    ☐ Misplaced or dangling modifiers

    ☐ Verb tense consistency

    ☐ Pronoun agreement

    ☐ Subject and verb agreement

Refer to Appendix A for a review of grammar concepts.

Final Assessment

☐ What do you like the most about the essay?

☐ What are you unclear about or have difficulty with in the essay?

APPENDIX A: Basic Grammar

If you are building a house, you will need sand, gravel, water, and cement to form the concrete foundation of your home. You may have these ingredients on hand, or you may have to go and find them. In writing, grammar rules are essential ingredients to the foundation of a good sentence, paragraph, or essay. You may have these rules already learned and ready to use—or you may have to go and find them. Many of the basic rules can be found in this appendix. Fuller explanations, exercises, and additional rules can be found in the companion to this book: *Building Better Grammar*. The definitions and rules are organized into three categories: completeness, consistency, and clarity.

I: BE COMPLETE

Parts of Speech

Every word you write or speak falls into one of eight categories or types. These are collectively called the **parts of speech**. The eight parts of speech are nouns, pronouns, verbs, adjectives, adverbs, prepositions, conjunctions, and interjections.

Nouns

The **noun** names a person, place, thing, or idea. Often, nouns are preceded by the article adjectives *the, a,* and *an.*

The <u>dog</u>
A <u>girl</u>

An <u>ant</u>
The <u>sky</u> is blue.
<u>Hurricanes</u> terrify me.
Their <u>belief</u> in the <u>right</u> of all <u>human beings</u> to live in <u>peace</u> is what motivates the <u>protestors</u>.

Pronouns

Pronouns take the place of nouns. They serve two functions:

1. **To avoid excessive repetition.**
   Manny calls Manny's teacher to tell the teacher that Manny will be late.
   Manny calls <u>his</u> teacher to tell <u>her</u> that <u>he</u> will be late.

2. **To refer to something or someone that is not specifically identified.**
   <u>Something</u> is bothering me.
   Why didn't you tell <u>anyone</u>?

The noun that a pronoun replaces is called the **antecedent**. Pronouns that refer to a clearly identified antecedent are called **definite pronouns**.

I, me, my, myself	he, him, his, himself
they, them, their, themselves	you, your, yourselves
she, her, hers, herself	we, us, our, ours, ourselves
who, whose, which, what	that, this, these, those
it, its, itself	

Pronouns that refer to a noun that is <u>not</u> clearly identified are called **indefinite pronouns**.

anything	nothing	something	everything
anyone	no one	someone	everyone
each	either	neither	many
few	some	must	

Verbs

Verbs show action or show a state of being.

Action verbs: some examples are *play, eat, talk, jump,* and *dance.*
   I <u>walk</u> home.
   The bells <u>jangled</u>.

Being verbs: these verbs are identified by the verb *to be: is, am, are, was, were, will be.*
   I <u>am</u> a mother.
   He <u>is</u> a monster.

Any of the forms of *be* (*am, is, was, were*) and also some other verbs can be used as **helping verbs**. Helping verbs come before the main verb to refine and clarify the exact nature and timing of the action.

He <u>is going</u> to the mall.

We <u>had helped</u> every time until now.

It <u>will be raining</u> soon.

Helping Verbs in Addition to *Be*			
do	does	did	have
has	had	shall	should
will	would	can	could
may	might	must	

Verbs change form according to when an action occurs; these changing verb forms are called **verb tenses**. Verb tenses help us track subjects and sentences in time:

Past	Present	Future
(All time before now)	(Now)	(All time beyond now)
The baby <u>talked</u>.	The baby <u>talks</u>.	The baby <u>will talk</u>.

Within each of these three tenses, there are four additional tenses that allow a writer to describe extremely specific times in which things happen. There are twelve tenses in all:

	Simple	Perfect	Progressive	Perfect Progressive
Present	She writes.	She has written.	She is writing.	She has been writing.
Past	She wrote.	She had written.	She was writing.	She had been writing.
Future	She will write.	She will have written.	She will be writing.	She will have been writing.

Adjectives and Adverbs

Adjectives and adverbs provide further description, identification, or limitation to the meaning of other words. They have similar properties, so adjectives and adverbs are often grouped together as **descriptors** or **modifiers**. What is the difference between them? **Adjectives** modify nouns and pronouns. They answer the questions: *Which one? What kind?* and *How many?*

The scientist photographed <u>red-winged</u> blackbirds.

I was delighted to see the <u>beautiful</u> blackbirds up close.

There were <u>ten</u> blackbirds.

Adverbs modify verbs, adjectives, and other adverbs, and they answer questions like *How? Where? When?* and *To what degree?*

He answered <u>quickly</u>.
They flew <u>south</u>.
The ship sailed <u>last week</u>.
She was <u>somewhat</u> angry.

Adjectives and adverbs come in three degrees: positive, comparative, and superlative. The **positive form** makes no comparison; the **comparative form** makes a comparison between two things; and the **superlative form** distinguishes among three or more things.

We go to an <u>old</u> school. (positive)
It is <u>older</u> than the state college. (comparative)
It is the <u>oldest</u> college in the Southwest. (superlative)

Prepositions

Prepositions are words that help signal a place (*above, inside, behind*), time (*before, after, within*), or source (*to, from, for, of, by*). Prepositions show the relationship between a noun or pronoun—called the **object** of the preposition—and other words in the sentence. Many words that are commonly used as prepositions may also function as adverbs or other parts of speech.

I looked <u>up</u> the street.
The bell rang <u>before</u> the teacher finished talking.
Did you get that <u>from</u> an online store?

Consult this list for more prepositions:

Place		Time	Source	
above	across	after	about	against
among	around	before	at	by
below	behind	during	because of	due to
beneath	beside	until	except	for
between	beyond	since	from	of
by	in/into		off	to
inside	near		toward	with
out	outside		without	
over	on			
through	under			
up	upon			
within				

Conjunctions

Conjunctions are words that join two or more clauses with one another. There are three kinds of conjunctions: coordinating, subordinating, and conjunctive adverbs.

1. **Coordinating conjunctions** link independent clauses. An easy way to remember these conjunctions is by using the acronym FANBOYS. The acronym includes the first letter of each of the seven coordinating conjunctions.

, for	and	, nor	, but	, or	, yet	, so

I like milk, <u>but</u> I prefer hot chocolate with breakfast.

2. **Subordinating conjunctions** link independent clauses with dependent clauses.

after	before	so that	whenever
although	because	provided that	where
as	even though	rather than	whereas
as if	if	until	whether
as long as	once	unless	while
as though	since	when	

I like my job <u>even though</u> I am not satisfied with the salary.
<u>Although</u> she is in pain, she is not letting it show.

3. **Adverbial conjunctions** link independent clauses.

; also,	; therefore,	; otherwise,	; consequently,
; besides,	; nonetheless,	; furthermore,	; nevertheless,
; instead,	; however,	; for instance,	; accordingly,
; indeed,	; moreover,	; likewise,	; for example,
; in fact,	; as a result,	; in addition,	; meanwhile,
; thus,	; then,	; similarly,	; hence,
; on the other hand,	; subsequently,		

He was finished with the project; <u>therefore</u>, he went home.

Interjections

Interjections are words that show surprise or emotion.
Hey, stop that please.
When an interjection appears alone, it is usually followed with an exclamation mark.
Wow!   Cowabunga!   Finally!

Parts of a Sentence

A sentence must contain a subject and a verb; without either one of these parts, a sentence is incomplete and will confuse the reader.

Subject

The **subject** is the part of the sentence that tells the reader who or what is doing or being something in the sentence.

Mary spoke.

[Mary is the subject of this sentence.]

Subjects can ONLY be nouns or pronouns, though these may be made up of multiple words.

The daughter of my father's best friend spoke.

Someone who shall remain nameless spoke.

Taken together, all the words that name or modify the subject are called the **complete subject**. There are three other ways to refer to a sentence's subject:

1. **Simple subject.** When a sentence has one noun or pronoun doing the action, that sentence has one subject known as a simple subject.

   Daniel plays the drums.

   Who plays the drums?

   Daniel ← 1 noun

   Because there is one subject, it is called a simple subject.

2. **Compound subject.** When a sentence has two or more nouns or pronouns doing the same action, they are collectively referred to as a compound subject.

   Daniel and Marty play the drums.

   Who plays the drums?

   Daniel and Marty ← 2 nouns

3. **Implied subject.** Sometimes a sentence does not directly state its subject, but it is clear that one exists.

   Come to the meeting to learn about the new tax laws.

   Here, the subject can be understood to be "you." Commands like this have the implied subject "you."

Verb

The second essential part of a sentence is the **verb**. Both the subject and verb can be one word or many.

1. The **simple verb** is the main verb of the sentence.

   Daniel plays the drums.

2. The **complete verb** includes not only the main verb but also all words that modify or directly relate to it.

   Daniel plays the drums fast enough to blow us away.

3. A **compound verb** occurs in a sentence where more than one verb has the same subject.
   > Daniel <u>plays</u> the drums, <u>writes</u> the songs, and <u>produces</u> the recordings.

Objects of Verbs

Some verbs require a **direct object**, a word or words that indicate who or what received the action of the verb.
> The record company pays its <u>songwriters</u> less than they deserve.

Without the direct object *songwriters* and its modifiers, this sentence—"The record company pays"—would be incomplete. You would ask, *Whom* or *what does the company pay?* Asking a *Whom?* or *What?* question about the verb of a sentence is a good way to find its direct object.

An **indirect object** is a person or thing to whom (or for whom) the action of the verb is directed. It must be a noun or a pronoun that comes before the direct object.
> Laura handed <u>Jerry</u> the keys.

(direct object=the keys; indirect object=Jerry)

To whom did Laura hand the keys? To Jerry. The keys is the direct object and Jerry is the indirect object of the verb *handed*.

Phrases

A phrase is a group of related words lacking a subject, a verb, or both. A phrase can function as a verb.
> Her family <u>has been having</u> a difficult year.

A phrase can function as a noun.
> <u>The board of trustees</u> blocked the motion.

A phrase can function as a modifier to the noun or verb.
> My mom, <u>a lifelong hypochondriac</u>, is in bed again. (phrase modifies noun)
> The new teacher arrived <u>long before the students</u>. (phrase modifies verb)

Clauses

It is important to understand the difference between a **sentence** and a **clause**. Both are grammatical labels for a group of words that <u>must</u> contain a subject and a verb. A sentence, however, <u>may</u> contain more than one subject/verb groups; in other words, a sentence may consist of one, two, or more clauses. Consider these examples:

I own a beautiful cat.	Number of sentences: 1 Number of clauses: 1
I own a beautiful cat; her fur is glossy black, and after I brush it, her eyes glow with pleasure and she snuggles in my arms with loud purrs of contentment.	Number of sentences: 1 Number of clauses: 4

You can break down the longer sentence into separate clauses by underlining the subject (noun or pronoun) and verb (action or state of being) in each clause.

I <u>own</u> a beautiful cat

her <u>fur is</u> glossy black

after <u>I brush</u> it

her <u>eyes glow</u> with pleasure

<u>she snuggles</u> in my arms with loud purrs of contentment

There are two kinds of clauses: independent and dependent. Learning to arrange and connect clauses of differing completeness and purpose will help you create and punctuate complex sentences without confusing your reader.

Independent Clauses

An **independent clause** has a subject and a verb and expresses a complete thought. As its name suggests, an independent clause is a complete sentence that can stand by itself and does not need more information to give it meaning.

Dan laughed.

Dan is the subject and *laughed* is the verb. Do you need to know more? Not really. You might want to know what made Dan laugh, where he is and who he is with, or whether his laugh was happy or bitter—but these pieces of information are not essential for understanding what the sentence means. Grammatically, all that matters is that the sentence has a subject and a verb and that it makes sense on its own. *Dan laughed,* therefore, is an independent clause.

Dependent Clauses

A **dependent clause** has a subject and a verb but does not express a complete thought. As its name suggests, a dependent clause is *dependent on* more information to give it meaning. It cannot stand on its own as a complete sentence. The dependent clause is also referred to as a subordinate clause since it starts with a subordinating conjunction.

When Dan laughs.

Although *Dan* is the subject and *laughs* is the verb, you need to know more to make a complete statement. What happens when Dan laughs? Does someone smile or get mad at him? Do other people join him? You need more information to complete the meaning of this clause. Adding another clause will provide the needed information.

When Dan laughs, the walls shake and the baby wakes up from his nap.

When Dan laughs, therefore, is a dependent clause. Notice that the dependent clause in the example was created by the addition of an opening word (*when*) which told the reader to wait for additional information.

Use these conjunctions to show logical relationships of meaning:

Addition:
and, both…and, also, besides, furthermore, moreover
Contrast:
but, yet, however, instead, nevertheless, otherwise, similarly
Choice:
or, nor, either…or
Effect:
so, accordingly, consequently, therefore, thus
Substitution:
not…but
Sequence:
first, meanwhile, next, then, finally
Emphasis:
indeed, certainly

Use these subordinating conjunctions to show logical relationships of meaning:

Cause and Effect:
as, because, since, so that, in order that, in order to
Condition:
if, even if, unless, if only
Contrast:
although, even though, though
Comparison:
than, as though, as if, whereas, while
Choice:
whether, than, rather than
Sequence:
after, as, as long as, as soon as, before, once, since, until, when, whenever, while
Space:
where, wherever
Time:
when, whenever

Kinds of Sentences

The Simple Sentence
A **simple sentence** consists of a single independent clause.

I ate cake.

A simple sentence never has more than one clause (subject + verb), but that clause may contain compound subjects and verbs.

T.J. and Richy ate all the cake.

Mona and the kids finished off the punch and cookies.

Everybody cleared the dishes, turned off the lights, and locked the door.

The Compound Sentence
A **compound sentence** contains two or more independent clauses. Each clause, when viewed alone, can stand on its own as a sentence without changes or additions.

I ate cake, and my girlfriend ate cookies.

[I ate cake] and [my girlfriend ate cookies.]

The independent clauses in a compound sentence can be joined together by the following two types of conjunctions: **coordinating** and **adverbial,** both of which require punctuation. You can also choose to join two independent clauses using a stand-alone semicolon.

I ate cake, but my girlfriend ate cookies. (comma + coordinating conjunction)

I ate cake; however, my girlfriend ate cookies. (comma + adverbial conjunction)

I ate cake; my girlfriend ate cookies. (semi-colon)

The Complex Sentence
The **complex sentence** consists of one independent clause and one or more dependent clauses. Remember that a dependent clause has a subject and a verb but does not express a complete thought; it cannot stand on its own as a complete sentence. Because a dependent clause by its very nature is subordinate or inferior to an independent clause, the only option for connecting clauses in a complex sentence is a **subordinating conjunction.** If the dependent clause comes before the independent clauses, separate the clauses with a comma.

If she has a choice between cookies and cake, my girlfriend will choose cookies.

(dependent clause + independent clause)

If the dependent clause follows an independent clause, NO comma is needed.

She will choose cookies if they contain chocolate chips.

(independent clause + dependent clause)

The Compound-Complex Sentence
The **compound-complex sentence** consists of two or more independent clauses and one or more dependent clauses.

My father encouraged me to pick up a hobby, so I started collecting stamps; I became rich when I started a company that acquires and sells rare stamps; consequently, my hobby is now my livelihood.

This sentence is really five simple sentences combined together through the use of conjunctions and a semicolon.

II: BE CONSISTENT

Subject-Verb Agreement

Because subjects and verbs must be present in every grammatically complete sentence, they have a strong relationship with one another. When the two elements do not agree, the sentence stumbles, as in these examples:

Dogs is my favorite animals.
Jim eat a hamburger nearly every day.
One of the most precious resources in the United States are water.

In each of these sentences, the subject and verb disagree in number. In order to agree, a verb must follow the form of its subject in number:

1. If the subject is singular, the verb must be singular.
   My brother plays football.
2. If the subject is plural, the verb must be plural.
   My brothers play football.

Notice that in both sample sentences only one –s appears:

My brother plays football.
My brothers play football.

As a general rule, a singular verb ends in –s; <u>a singular noun does not</u>; a plural noun ends in –s; <u>a plural verb does not</u>.

This rule applies, however, only to regular verbs. Irregular verbs change form entirely according to number and person. The most troublesome irregular verbs for subject-verb agreement are *to be*, *to do*, and *to have*.

Irregular Verb Subject-Verb Agreement					
To be		**To do**		**To have**	
Present	**Past**	**Present**	**Past**	**Present**	**Past**
I am	I was	I do	I did	I have	I had
You are	You were	You do	You did	You have	You had
He/she/ it is	He/she/ it was	He/she/ it does	He/she/ it did	He/she/ it has	He/she/ it had
We are	We were	We do	We did	We have	We had
They are	They were	They do	They did	They have	They had

To be successful at subject-verb agreement, always locate the subject first and determine its number, then judge whether the present tense verb agrees with it. If the subject is singular, the verb should have an –s added to it to match its singular form. If the subject is plural (often ending in –s), the verb should not have an –s.

1. **Singular subjects can be:**
   a. Simple or singular.
      A student (talk, talks).
      He or she talks.
      A student talks.
   b. A collective noun. Test by replacing it with the pronoun *it*.
      The team (play, plays).
      It plays.
      The team plays.
   c. Subjects stating amount (time, money, measurement, weight, volume, fractions) are usually singular when the amount is considered as a unit. Test by replacing with the singular pronoun *it*.
      Six dollars (is, are) enough for the movie.
      It is enough.
      Six dollars is enough.
   d. An indefinite pronoun—*everyone, everybody, everything,* and *each.* Test by replacing it with the singular pronouns *he/she/it.*
      Each student (talk, talks).
      He or she talks.
      Each student talks.

2. **Plural subjects can be:**
   a. Simple and plural. Test by replacing with the plural pronouns *we* or *they.*
      The students (talk, talks).
      We talk.
      They talk.
      The students talk.
   b. Compound (two or more subjects). Test by replacing with the plural pronoun *they.*
      The students and the teacher (talk, talks).
      They talk.
      The students and the teacher talk.

c. An indefinite pronoun—*several, few, both, many.* Test by replacing it with the plural pronouns *we/they.*

Many (talk, talks).

We talk.

They talk.

Many talk.

Pronoun-Antecedent Agreement

Just as a verb must agree with its subject, so a pronoun must agree with the noun it replaces. That noun—called the **antecedent**—has a recognizable point of view, number, and gender. The pronoun reference has to agree with the **person, number,** or **gender** of the antecedent.

Pronoun Agreement with Person

If the antecedent is a person, then agreement can be achieved by using the pronouns *he* or *she.* If the antecedent is about the second person *(you),* then agreement can be achieved by using the pronoun *you.* If the antecedent is a thing, then agreement can be achieved by using the pronoun *it.*

If a person wants to succeed in this game, he or she must know the rules.

If you want to succeed in this game, you must know the rules.

For this game to be successful, it needs to have specific rules.

Use the same person throughout a sentence. Throughout the discussion, maintain the point of view that begins the sentence or the text.

Inconsistent: You must be careful when you hike because the consequences could be deadly for him or her.

Consistent: You must be careful when you hike because the consequences could be deadly for you.

Pronoun Agreement with Number

If the antecedent is plural, the pronoun(s) must also be plural; if the antecedent is singular, the pronoun(s) must also be singular.

If people want to succeed in this game, they must know the rules.

If Kayla wants to succeed in this game, she must learn the rules.

The number agreement is most confusing when a sentence includes an indefinite pronoun or a collective noun.

1. **Indefinite pronouns are pronouns that do not indicate a definite person or thing.** Here is a list of some common indefinite pronouns:

everybody	everyone	everything	each
anybody	anyone	anything	either
somebody	someone	something	neither
nobody	no one	nothing	

Whenever these pronouns are used in a sentence, a singular pronoun (he/she or his/her) is required to refer back to them.

Incorrect:	**Everyone** must turn in **their** work.
Correct:	**Everyone** must turn in **his or her** work.
Incorrect:	**Each** of the boys brought **their** book.
Correct:	**Each** of the boys brought **his** book.
Incorrect:	Someone left **their** folder behind.
Correct:	Someone left **his/her** folder behind.

Some writers and speakers have a tendency to use the plural *their* as the reference pronoun to indefinite pronouns. This seems like an easy way to avoid the historically sexist practice of always using *his* when referring to a general person. However, since these indefinite pronouns emphasize a single body, one, or thing, the singular pronouns *he, she, his, her,* or *it* must be used.

2. **Collective nouns, such as army, team, or committee, sound plural but in reality are singular units composed of many elements.** For example, a team is a single unit made up of many players. Because it is still a "single" unit, it requires the singular pronoun *it* for reference.

The **army** deployed **its** recruits.
The **team** played **its** final game.

Pronoun Agreement with Gender

A pronoun has to agree with the masculine or feminine state of the antecedent. When a pronoun refers to a singular female noun, the pronoun must be gender-specific (*she, her*).

The **girl** turned in **her** assignment.

When a pronoun refers to a singular male noun, the pronoun must be gender-specific (*he, his*).

The **man** walked **his** dog.

Parallelism

Whenever you use a single part of speech two or more times in a sentence, each use must consistently present the part of speech in the same form. **Parallelism** in writing means that similar elements or ideas in a sentence are presented in the same form grammatically, so the reader can quickly grasp the comparison or connection being made between them. The need for parallel construction arises when your sentence contains **pairs** (two items); **lists** (three or more items); **comparisons using *than* or *as***; and **paired expressions**.

Parallelism with Pairs and Lists

You can spot pairs (two items) in sentences when you see the words *and, or.* When you use these two words, everything that comes before the *and/or* must present the same grammatical form as everything that comes after the *and/or.* The following sentences fail to achieve that balance.

I returned three books to the library <u>and</u> checking out two more.

I will drive to the library <u>or</u> rode the bus.

You need to change one of the sides to make the sentence parallel.

Correct: I returned three books to the library and checked out two more.

Correct: I will drive to the library or ride the bus.

Multiple options exist for creating parallelism in any sentence. Look at another example:

He dances <u>skillfully</u> and <u>with gracefulness</u>.

Here, the adverb *skillfully* comes before the *and* while the noun *gracefulness* comes after the *and.* The sentence will not achieve parallelism until one of these modifiers is changed.

Correct: He dances skillfully and gracefully. [adverb / adverb]

Correct: He dances with skill and grace. [noun / noun]

Parallelism must be achieved whenever pairs or lists occur in a sentence, no matter what parts of speech are involved. Here are some rules to keep in mind for specific parts of speech:

1. **Pairs and lists of verbs must be parallel in tense.**

    Incorrect: On my birthday, we sang, danced, and were eating.

    The list in this example starts with a past tense of the verb *sang;* all the verbs listed after *sang,* therefore, should also be in the past tense. *Were eating* is in the progressive past; hence, this sentence is not parallel. To correct the sentence, either change *were eating* to *ate* or change all the other verbs to past progressive.

    Correct: On my birthday, we sang, danced, and ate.

    Correct: On my birthday, we were singing, dancing, and eating.

    Note: In any list of items, be sure to use commas between each item.

2. **Pairs and lists of nouns must be parallel in number, person, and kind.**

    Incorrect: I bought coffee, some tea, and two pounds of sugar.

    The list in this example starts with a noun that has no designated measurement, followed by two nouns that do have designated measurements. This list lacks parallelism. To correct it, either add measurements to all the nouns or remove the measurements from all the nouns.

Correct: I bought coffee, tea, and sugar.

Correct: I bought one pound of coffee, two pounds of tea, and five pounds of sugar.

3. **Pairs and lists of adjectives must be parallel in form.**

Incorrect: The race was dangerous, creative, and had much excitement.

The list in this example has an adjective *(had much excitement)* which does not parallel the form of the other two adjectives in the sentence. Hence, this list is not parallel. To correct this sentence, reduce the last adjective to one word.

Correct: The race was a dangerous, creative, and exciting.

Parallelism with Comparisons (Than or Avs)

To make comparisons, you must use the words *than* or *as*. When you edit for parallelism, make sure that the things being compared on either side of those words are parallel.

Incorrect: Driving to school is better <u>than to take</u> the bus.

The verbs on either side of *than* are not presented in the same tense. You must change one or the other to make the sentence parallel.

Correct: Driving to school is better <u>than taking</u> the bus.

Correct: <u>To drive</u> to school is better <u>than to take</u> the bus.

Parallelism with Paired Expressions

Paired expressions—also called correlative conjunctions—require parallel structure. These five sets of conjunctions are always paired:

Both...and

Either...or

Neither...nor

Not only...but also or but too

Rather...than

Achieve parallel construction when using paired expressing by presenting the words that follow the first conjunction in the same format as the words that follow the second conjunction.

Incorrect: I want <u>both</u> to be wealthy <u>and</u> health.

Correct: I want <u>both</u> wealth <u>and</u> health.

Correct: I want <u>both</u> to be wealthy <u>and</u> to be healthy.

Incorrect: <u>Either</u> we go to the park <u>or</u> we are going to the mountains.

Correct: <u>Either</u> we go to the park <u>or</u> we go to the mountains.

Correct: <u>Either</u> we are going to the park <u>or</u> we are going to the mountains.

Incorrect: He can <u>neither</u> tell his boss the truth <u>nor</u> to quit his job.

Correct: He can <u>neither</u> tell his boss the truth <u>nor</u> quit his job.

Incorrect: Sugar is used <u>not only</u> in cakes <u>but</u> to make paste.

Correct: Sugar is used <u>not only</u> in cakes <u>but</u> also in paste.

Correct: Sugar is used <u>not only</u> to make cakes <u>but</u> also to make paste.

Incorrect: They would <u>rather</u> eat out <u>than</u> to be eating their father's cooking.

Correct: They would <u>rather</u> eat out <u>than</u> eat their father's cooking.

Tense Consistency

You use verbs every time you write a sentence. Although the actions that take place in your paragraphs may show movement between different times, keeping to one verb tense within each sentence, paragraph, and in the overall work will avoid confusion and will help the reader follow more clearly what you are saying. To achieve this consistency, make all the verbs in the same tense as the first verb you used in the sentence.

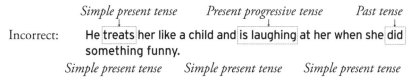

Incorrect: He treats her like a child and is laughing at her when she did something funny.

Correct: He treats her like a child and laughs at her when she does something funny.

OR

He is treating her like a child and is laughing at her when she is doing something funny.

III: BE CLEAR

Punctuation

Commas

Commas signal brief pauses, which help readers understand the flow of thought or action in a sentence. Beginning writers may use either too few or too many commas, so their sentences are unclear or difficult to read. Commas are used for two purposes: to separate and to enclose.

Commas Used to Separate

Commas create a small but necessary amount of separation between items on a list and phrases that introduce or lead up to an independent clause. They are also used to create a necessary pause between two independent clauses, allowing readers time to separate and compare them in their minds.

1. **Commas and items in a list.**

   Use commas to separate items in a list (three or more items). This includes the last item in the series which usually has either the word *and*, or the word *or* before it.

Series of nouns:	I bought coffee, tea, flour, and sugar.
Series of verbs:	At the meeting, I ate, drank, and mingled with my supervisors.

2. **Commas and introductory expressions.**

   An introductory expression is a phrase composed of one word (*finally, oh, however*) or a group of words (*by the end of the day* or *as we all know*). It comes at the beginning of a sentence, and it never contains the subject and verb that create the basic meaning of the sentence. In other words, if you were to take an introductory expression out of the sentence, the remaining part of the sentence would make sense on its own. Use a comma after an introductory expression to let your readers know which part of the sentence is the main one or the one that makes sense on its own.

   <u>Nonetheless</u>, I must take this in to the inspector.
   <u>By the way</u>, I spoke to Tim today.
   <u>According to Mr. Smith</u>, the case is about to be closed.

3. **Commas and conjunctions.**

   There are three types of conjunctions, and with each type, you must use commas in different locations to separate the clauses.

   - **Coordinating conjunctions** join two independent clauses and require a comma before the conjunction.

     John finished his essay, <u>but</u> Brian is still working on his.

   - **Adverbial conjunctions** join two or more independent clauses and require a semicolon before the conjunction and a comma after the conjunction.

     Kim went to the party; <u>however</u>, she did not stay long.

   - **Subordinating conjunctions** join an independent clause with a dependent clause and require a comma only if the conjunction is at the beginning of the sentence.

<u>When</u> I got home, I saw the mess the robbers had left behind.
[Comma needed]
I saw the mess the robbers had left behind <u>when</u> I got home.
[No comma needed]

Commas to Enclose

Words or phrases that are not essential to the basic understanding of a sentence must be enclosed, or surrounded, by commas.

1. **Commas and interrupters.** An interrupter is a word or a group of words that appears in the middle of the sentence but which, like an introductory expression, does not contain the subject or verb necessary to the basic meaning of the sentence. Interrupters might be called "scoopables" as a way of thinking about their purpose in a sentence—the words can be scooped out of the sentence without changing the basic meaning of the sentence. Interrupters may separate the subject and the verb and may break the sentence's flow—sometimes for dramatic effect—but they do not add to or subtract from the basic grammatical meaning.

   Use commas before and after an interrupter to enclose or set off the "scoopable" from the subject and verb of the sentence.

   I must take this, <u>nonetheless</u>, and show it to the inspector.
   I spoke to Tim, <u>by the way</u>, and he agreed to come.
   The criminal case, <u>according to Mr. Smith</u>, is about to be closed.

2. **Commas and direct address.** When the speaker in a sentence talks to another person and names that person, the process is called direct address because the speaker is directly addressing his or her audience. Put commas around the name that appears in the sentence.

   <u>John</u>, may I stop by your office today?
   I think, <u>Jim</u>, you are mistaken about the situation.
   Your grades are excellent, <u>Manny</u>!

   Note: If the name is the subject in the sentence, do not separate the subject from the verb with a comma unless there is an interrupter.

   Incorrect: **John, is my friend.**
   Correct: **John is my friend.**

Here, the sentence is talking *about* John, not to John, so the name is the subject in the sentence, and the subject cannot be separated from the verb with a comma.

3. **Commas with dates and addresses.**

   a. Use a comma to separate the month and day from the year.
      I was born on November 15, 2001.

      November 15 is one day out of 365 days of the calendar year 2001. That is, it is one day inside of that year, so a comma is needed to separate the day from the year and to indicate that the specific day falls inside that specific year.
      Also, if you include the name of a day in your date, separate it from the other elements with a comma.

      I was elected on Tuesday, November 4, 2008.

      Note: Do not use a comma if just the month and year are given.

      I was elected in November 2008.

   b. Use a comma to separate elements of an address included in a sentence or to separate the city from the state.

      I live on 100 W. Pine Street, Covina, California 91520.
      I lived in Dallas, Texas.

      Note: No comma is needed between the state and zip code.

Apostrophes

The **apostrophe** is a mark that looks exactly like a comma but is raised and placed between letters in a word rather than between whole words. Apostrophes allow you to write more efficiently, with fewer words, in two specific situations:

1. **To show possession.** An apostrophe allows you to take a wordy sentence like *The jacket belongs to Jim,* and shorten into the phrase *Jim's jacket.* Whenever you need to show that something or someone owns or possesses something or someone else, <u>always</u> use an apostrophe and <u>sometimes</u> add an *–s*. Grammar has established clear rules for how to tell when you need to add the *–s*:

   a. To show ownership with singular nouns, use the apostrophe and *–s*.

      Jim's jacket   **Girl's coat**   **Jess's hat**
      Everybody's turn   **Anyone's question**

   b. To show possession or ownership with plural nouns that do not end in *–s* or *–es*, use an apostrophe and add an *–s*.

      Men's cologne   **People's concern**   **Children's clothing**

   c. To show possession with plural nouns ending with *–s*, use only an apostrophe.

      Girls' coats   **Teams' coaches**

d. When two nouns are involved, apostrophes must show whether the subjects have joint or individual ownership.

My brother and sister's car (they share the same car)
My brother's and sister's cars (they each own a separate car)

e. To show possession with personal pronouns, do not use an apostrophe at all.

Yours is my favorite painting in the gallery.
Whose wallet is this?

2. **To show contractions.** Contractions are handy for shortening or contracting two words into one. Use an apostrophe to indicate the position of the missing letter or letters. The following verbs are often used in a contracted form:

Verbs with *not*	can not = can't	was not = wasn't
	are not = aren't	do not = don't
Pronouns with *will*	I will = I'll	she will = she'll
	you will = you'll	they will = they'll
Pronouns and nouns with the verb *to be*	it is = it's	who is = who's
	I am = I'm	Mark is = Mark's
Pronouns with *would*	I would = I'd	we would = we'd
	he would = he'd	they would = they'd

Note: One special contraction changes letters as well as drops them: *Will not* becomes *won't* in the contracted form.

3. **To form the plurals of letters and figures.**

Cross your t's.   **Her p's and q's all look the same.**

Spelling

To become a better speller, always proofread your writing and follow five important strategies.

Proofreading

Proofreading is checking a piece of writing for accuracy and correctness. Its purpose is to catch any careless mistakes that might distract or confuse readers. Proofreading is best done after all substantial changes, improvements, and additions have been made to the paper. Try the following techniques:

- Print out your writing and proofread on hard copy.
- Read your paper aloud.
- Ask someone else to read your paper aloud, and listen carefully as he or she reads.
- Run your writing through a spell-check program.

■ Read your text backward. Turn to the last line of your paper, hold a ruler or pencil over the line just above, and move it up as you read from the bottom up, checking one word at a time.

Spelling Strategies

1. **Create spelling lists.** Create a list of words you have trouble with and update the list as you encounter new words. Check to see whether a word that you find troublesome shares a root, prefix, or suffix with a word you already know; the connection helps you learn the meaning, as well as the spelling, of the new word.

2. **Learn the ei/ie rule.** Write *i* before *e* except after *c* (or when it sounds like *a* as in neighbor or weigh).

i before *e*:	chief	piece	brief	yield	priest
after *c*:	ceiling	receive	receipt	perceive	deceive
sounds like *a*:	eight	freight	vein	their	neighbor

Note: Four exceptions exist to this rule: *leisure, seizure, foreign,* and *height* all have *ei* spellings, though none of the four come after *c* or sound like *a*.

3. **Know commonly misspelled words.** Many words are misspelled because of their unusual letter combinations or incorrect pronunciation. Study this list to strengthen your ability to spot and avoid misspellings:

Incorrect	Correct
sincerly	sincerely
fourty	forty
libary	library
payed	paid
judgement	judgment
coperate	cooperate
goverment	government
seperate	separate
necesary	necessary
privaledge	privilege

4. **Know commonly confused words.** Words that sound alike or look alike can cause frequent spelling errors. Here's a list of confusing pairs of words.

Accept: to receive (verb)   I accept your decision.
Except: other than (preposition)   I greeted everyone except you.

Advice: guidance (noun)
Advise: to give guidance (verb)

I like your advice.
She advised me to drop the
class.

Affect: to influence (verb)
Effect: result (noun)

The pollution affects our lungs.
Pollution has a strong effect on
our lungs.

All ready: all (pronoun) are ready
(adverb)
Already: before (adverb)

The passengers were all ready
to board the ship.
I did this assignment already.

Brake: to stop (verb)
Break: to come apart (verb)

The train brakes at railroad signs.
That vase breaks easily.

Capital: city or money (noun)

Sacramento is the capital of
California.
He raised capital for his busi-
ness venture.

Capitol: a building (noun)

Washington has a capitol
building.

Clothes: apparel (noun)
Cloths: fabric (plural noun)

I wear my clothes.
My clothes are made from cloths.

Conscience: moral guide (noun)
Conscious: awake or aware
(adverb)

Lies are against my conscience.
The accident victim was not
conscious.

Desert: dry land (noun)
Dessert: sweet food (noun)

The desert climate is hot.
Apple pie is a great dessert.

Heard: past tense of *to hear* (verb)
Herd: a group of animals (noun)

I heard a rumor about the war.
The herd of cows is let out.

Knew: past tense of *to know* (verb)
New: recent, not old (adjective)

I knew a sweet man.
My new boots squeak.

Loose: not too tight (adjective)
Lose: not to win (verb)

My pants are loose on my waist.
I always lose at Scrabble.

Personal: private (adjective)
Personnel: employees
(plural noun)

This is a personal matter.
The personnel at the company
are frustrated.

Principal: leader (noun)	She is the principal of our school.
Principle: rule or concept (noun)	America is based on the principle of democracy.
Quite: entirely or very (adverb)	The dress is quite lovely.
Quiet: silent (adjective)	He is a quiet person.
Quit: to stop (verb)	I quit my job.
Then: next in time (adverb)	We danced then ate.
Than: to compare (conjunction)	He is shorter than Doris.
Thought: past tense of *to think* (verb)	I thought of him always.
Though: form of *although* (conjunction)	Though he is gone, I still love him.
Weather: climate (noun)	The weather is cold.
Whether: either or in case (conjunction)	We should know whether it will rain tonight.

5. **Know the word endings.** Sometimes, the spelling error occurs in how we spell the end of a word. This occurs most commonly when we are changing a word from the singular to the plural form. Here are a few guidelines to keep in mind:

- For words ending in *s, ss, x, z, sh,* or *ch* add an *–es.*

boxes	churches	mistresses	fizzes	dishes

- For words ending in *f* or *fe,* change the *f* to *y* and add *–es.*

shelf	shelves	wife	wives

- For words ending in *o* preceded by a vowel (*a,e,i,o,u*) add *–s.* For words ending in *o* preceded by a consonant, add *–es.*

with vowels:	zoo	zoos	rodeo	rodeos
with consonant:	hero	heroes	tomato	tomatoes

- For words ending in *y,* change the *y* to *i* and add *–es.*

city	cities	lily	lilies	candy	candies

- For some words, no ending is required to show the plural form.

fish	sheep	series	deer

- For some words, we change the whole word, not just the ending.

child	children	man	men	tooth	teeth

- For Greek and Latin nouns, there are special spellings to show plural form.

datum	data	thesis	theses	criterion
syllabus	syllabi	analysis	analyses	criteria

Common Sentence Errors

Fragments

A complete sentence must contain both a subject and a verb. A **fragment** is an incomplete sentence that does not make sense and cannot stand on its own. A fragment has one of the following five problems.

1. **The sentence is missing a subject.**
   Can't be my friend. (fragment)
   <u>Tom</u> cannot be my friend. (complete sentence)

   Remember that a subject can be a person, place, thing, or idea.

   Doesn't have to lead to bitter fights. (fragment)
   <u>Expressing a political opinion</u> doesn't have to lead to bitter fights.
   (complete sentence)

   A subject can also be a pronoun.

   <u>This</u> does not have to lead to bitter fights. (complete sentence)

2. **The sentence is missing a verb.**
   The girl in the red hood. (fragment)
   The girl with the red hood <u>walked</u> toward me. (complete sentence)

   Remember that a verb can be a state of being as well as an action.

   Unselfish love toward another human being. (fragment)
   Unselfish love toward another human being <u>is rare</u>. (complete sentence)

3. **The sentence is missing both a subject and a verb.**
   At the end of the day. (fragment)
   On the soccer field. (fragment)
   To play the piano. (fragment)

   To fix the fragment, add an independent clause (which by definition contains both a subject and a verb) to the phrase.

   At the end of the day, <u>Gina watches the sun set</u>. (complete sentence)
   <u>The players cheered</u> on the soccer field. (complete sentence)
   <u>I am longing</u> to play the piano. (complete sentence)

4. **The sentence is missing a helping verb.** The sentence has an *–ing* verb with no helping verb (*is, are, was, were, has, have, had…*).

   Barry running to the door. (fragment)

   To fix the fragment, add a helping verb.

   Barry <u>kept</u> running to the door. (complete sentence)

5. **The sentence is a dependent clause which cannot stand alone.** Even though it contains both a subject and a verb, a dependent clause does not express a complete thought.

   When the band started to play. (fragment)

   While she talked on the phone. (fragment)

   That Jerry described. (fragment)

   To fix the fragment, add an independent clause.

   When the band started to play, <u>people got up to dance.</u> (complete sentence)

   <u>Jerry interrupted her</u> while she talked on the phone. (complete sentence)

   <u>She couldn't understand the directions</u> that Jerry described. (complete sentence)

Run-ons

Run-ons, also called run-together sentences, are sentence errors made up of two side-by-side independent clauses that have no punctuation between them. The lack of punctuation makes it difficult for a reader to follow the movement from one complete thought to the other.

   We did not hear about the party until Friday we had to quickly change our plans.

Placing a conjunction between the two clauses helps but is still difficult to follow.

   We did not hear about the party until Friday <u>so</u> we had to quickly change our plans.

Punctuation must also be added to create a big enough pause for the reader's brain to correctly understand the sentence:

   We did not hear about the party till Friday<u>, so</u> we had to quickly change our plans.

To fix run-ons, use one of the following solutions:

1. **Add a period between the two independent clauses.**

   We didn't hear about the party until Friday<u>.</u> We had to change our plans.

2. **Add a semicolon between the two independent clauses.**

   We had to change our plans<u>;</u> we didn't hear about the party until Friday.

3. **Add a conjunction and punctuate correctly.**

    a. , + coordinating conjunction

      We didn't hear about the party until Friday, <u>so</u> we had to change our plans.

    b. ; + adverbial conjunction + ,

      We didn't hear of the party until Friday; <u>therefore,</u> we changed our plans.

    c. subordinating conjunction with or without comma

      <u>When</u> we heard about the party, we changed our plans.

      We changed our plans <u>when</u> we heard about the party.

Comma Splices

Comma splices are sentence errors made up of two side-by-side independent clauses with only a comma separating them. The comma interrupts the reader's movement from one complete thought to the other.

    The storm hit sooner than expected, the race was cancelled.

Placing a conjunction between the two clauses helps, but it is still difficult to follow if the conjunction is not punctuated correctly.

    The storm hit sooner than expected <u>yet,</u> the race was cancelled.

The conjunction must be added in the right place relative to the comma, so a big enough pause is created for the reader's brain to correctly understand the sentence.

    The storm hit sooner than expected, <u>yet</u> the race was cancelled.

To fix comma splices, use one of the following solutions:

1. **Add a period between the two independent clauses.**

    The storm hit sooner than expected. The race was cancelled.

2. **Add a semicolon between the two independent clauses.**

    The storm hit sooner than expected; the race was cancelled.

3. **Add a conjunction and punctuate correctly.**

    a. , + coordinating conjunction

      The storm hit sooner than expected, <u>and</u> the race was cancelled.

    b. ; + adverbial conjunction + ,

      The storm hit sooner than expected; <u>consequently,</u> the race was cancelled.

    c. subordinating conjunction with or without comma

      <u>Since</u> the storm hit sooner than expected, the race was cancelled.

      The storm hit sooner than expected <u>before</u> the race was cancelled.

APPENDIX B: Commonly Used Transitions

GENERAL

certainly	indeed	no doubt
in addition	in fact	moreover
of course	to be sure	also
furthermore	next	then
besides		

NARRATION

recently	previously	earlier
meanwhile	at the same time	soon/soon after
next	the next day	finally
in the past	now/by now	suddenly
later	then	eventually
in the end		

DESCRIPTION

above/on top	beneath/under	ahead/in front of
behind/in back of	toward	away from
near	close by	at hand
across from	beside	nearby
in the middle	in the center	in the distance
to the left, to the right	next to	between

EXAMPLES

one example	another example	most important example
for instance	in other words	namely
an illustration of this is	a case in point	one such case
for example	specifically	to illustrate
a typical case		

EFFECT

first effect	second effect	most important effect
as a result	thus	therefore
consequently		

CAUSE

first reason	second reason	most important reason
one reason	another reason	because
accordingly	then	so

COMPARISON

as well	equally	likewise
similarly		

CONTRAST

however	in contrast	instead
on the contrary	as opposed to	on the other hand
nevertheless	unlike	

ARGUMENT

I propose	I agree
because	since
the opposition would have you believe	although there are those who
some may claim	we have been told that
consequently	as a result
an additional reason	while it is true
a convincing piece of evidence	in view of this fact
popular thought is that	therefore

EMPHASIS/IMPORTANCE

clearly	above all	in fact
most of all	most	undoubtedly
in particular	indeed	least of all
especially	importantly	

SPACE

above	at the back	behind
closer in	farther out	in front
inside	nearby	on the bottom
on the left/right	on top	outside
below	beside	in the middle
under		

TIME

after that	at that time	at the moment
eventually	first	gradually
in the future	in the past	later
presently	so far	suddenly
currently	earlier	immediately
meanwhile	now	one day
then	these days	nowadays

CONCLUSION

generally	in other words	in short
thus	on the whole	therefore

APPENDIX C: Quotation Protocol

HOW TO INTEGRATE QUOTATIONS

When using quotations, they should be integrated into your own sentences. Don't drop quotations into your text without warning, and avoid standing quotations alone as sentences; instead, provide clear **signal phrases** that include the author's name, to prepare readers for the quotation:

> According to oncologist John Shepard, "The bald eagle has stabilized its population."

Here are other examples to vary your signal phrases:

> In the words of author Ron Reel, "...
> As Fiona Davis has noted, "...
> The Stones point out, "...
> Sociologist Sid Maynard offers this argument for this theory: "...

Use **active verbs** in signal phrases to indicate the author's stance. Provided here are some verbs that you could use:

acknowledges	comments	describes	maintains	report	claims
adds	compares	disputes	notes	responds	denies
admits	conceded	emphasizes	observes	shows	writes
agrees	confirms	endorses	points out	states	insists
argues	contends	illustrates	reasons	suggests	rejects
asserts	declares	implies	refutes	summarizes	

MLA CONVENTIONS FOR QUOTING PROSE

For quotations of less than four lines, place quoted language in quotation marks and incorporate into your text:

> The prisoner steps slightly aside to avoid a puddle, and Orwell observes, "It is curious, but till that moment I had never realized what it means to destroy a healthy, conscious man."

For variety, you can also divide the quotations by working the signal phrase into the middle of the sentence:

> "It is curious," Orwell notes, as the prisoner steps slightly aside to avoid a puddle, "but till that moment I had never realized what it means to destroy a healthy, conscious man."

Or, you can work parts (phrases or key words) of the original quotation into your sentence:

> Orwell finds it "curious" that until his involvement in the hanging of a Burmese prisoner he "had never realized what it means to destroy a healthy, conscious man."

For longer quotations four lines or more set the passage off from your text by starting a new line indented one inch, and do not attach quotation marks.

> Orwell describes the prisoner not as a dying man but as a man who is alive:
> All the organs of his body were working—all toiling away in solemn foolery. His nails would still be growing when he stood on the drop, when he was falling through the air with a tenth of a second to live. His eyes saw the yellow gravel and the grey walls, and his brain still remembered, foresaw, and reasoned.

When you wish to omit a portion of the original quoted language, use an ellipsis to signal to the reader that you have edited the original.

> Orwell reports, "His eyes saw the yellow gravel and the grey walls. . . reasoned about puddles."
> Orwell reports, "His eyes saw the yellow gravel and the grey wall . . . ."

(add a 4th point to the ellipsis if it ends the sentence.)

> Orwell reports, ". . . his brain remembered, foresaw, and reasoned."

Index